Seeking

HOA CONSTITUTIONAL GOVERNMENT:

the continuing battle

Collected Writings

GEORGE K. STAROPOLI

"Democracies may die at the hands of elected leaders; [they] erode slowly, in barely visible steps. There is no single moment in which the regime obviously 'crosses the line' into dictatorship by using the institutions of democracy to kill it." *(How Democracies Die*, Steven Levitsky & Daniel Ziblatt)

"CIDS [HOAs] currently engage in many activities that would be prohibited if they were viewed by the courts as the equivalent of local governments."
(Evan McKenzie, *Privatopia*)

CC&Rs are a devise for de facto HOA governments to escape constitutional government

StarMan Publishing

Seeking

HOA CONSTITUTIONAL GOVERNMENT:

the continuing battle

Collected Writings

George K. Staropoli
George@pvtgov.org http://pvtgov.org http://pvtgov.info

Published by
StarMan Publishing
15767 W. Silver Breeze Dr.
Surprise, AZ 85374-5041

ISBN: 978-0-9744488-8-6

Printed in the United States of America

LEGAL DISCLAIMER

The author has made every effort to be factual and has obtained materials believed to be factual or are the opinions of the writer, and from sources deemed to be reliable. This publication is being distributed with the expressed and implied understanding that the editor and publisher are not engaged in rendering legal, accounting, or other professional advice.

Preface

The posts contained herein have been selected from my Commentaries posted in HOA Constitutional Government (http://pvtgov.info). There are over 1,300 posts dating back to 2004 discussing issues, and dealing with events, legislation, statutes, and state court appellate cases that came to my attention. The Commentaries are short, to the point, and contain related notes, references, and links to complete papers and provide authoritative documents for further study. They are the original Commentaries with some technical adaptations.

A few words about format. Links are displayed in blue and underlined. However, due to the time of the post many links may result in a *not found* message. The link's web page has been removed or deleted by the author beyond my control. This is unfortunate, especially in the instance of CAI and many news reports. Quoted material is shown as indented paragraphs or by italicized quotes within a sentence. Terms or words emphasized or being given special meaning are shown as italicized.

An online PDF version of this *Collected Writings* is available to purchasers of the book. The link is provided in the purchased copy:
http://pvtgov.org/pvtgov/downloads/collected-writings.pdf.

I would like to acknowledge the people with whom I had discussions and worked with over the years making my journey possible. In Arizona: Clink Bolick, Tim Hogan, Eddie Farnsworth, Nancy Barto, Karen (Potts) Mullins, Dr. Jack Potts, and Steve Cheifetz. Across the country there were: Deborah Goonan (PA), Shu Bartholomew (VA), Julio Robaina (FL), David Khane (TX), Donie Vanitzian (CA), Elizabeth McMahon (CA), Frank Askin (NJ), Beanie Adolph (TX), Fred Pilot (CA), Bill Breetze (CT), and Steven Seigel (NJ).

December 23, 2023

Recommended Authors For You by AMAZON

Follow to get new release updates and improved recommendations

Peter F. Drucker

Bob Woodward

Introduction

And the Land Shall Be Made Good Again
George K. Staropoli

In the beginning There was the land,
And the land was good And the people were happy.

Soon upon the land Came the moneychangers
In the guise of builders Of the community.

And the moneychangers said, Behold, the covenants,
conditions
and restrictions
Were sacred and holy works, And the people shall flourish
and
prosper.

And the legislatures looked upon these CC&Rs And said
they were
sacred and holy,
And that land values shall multiply ten-fold, And the people
shall flourish and prosper.

But the moneychangers were not content, Seeking laws that
forced the people
Against their judgment and wishes Into mandated planned

communities.

Soon, the multitude became angry at their plight,
Yet the moneychangers and legislature
Cast the people into involuntary servitudes With continued tithes while disputes
went unresolved.

The child-like people, seeking paradise On earth and the gates of heaven,
Were not permitted audiences With the magistrates.

And so the multitude suffered A long and terrible time,
Praying for a savior one day To deliver them from their existence.

One sect sought the accommodation With the ruling powers and
moneychangers.
Another sought a cleansing Of an unworkable oppression upon the people.

Those seeking accommodation held fast to their desires
To see their fortunes on earth multiply ten-fold,
And that all such plans were good and just, For the land values
increased for all the community.

But many saw the desecration of the beliefs, values and ideals
Of the founders of the Great Nation that covered the land,
Saying behold the society that thou hast created,

Where Me First has replaced Love Thy Neighbor.

A babble of communities arose By the followers of the moneychangers,
With beliefs, values and ideals of the Old Ways, Once rejected by the Founders of the Great Nation.

Woe unto the followers of the moneychangers For the sins of the fathers shall be cast upon the sons.
Repent now and restore the beliefs, values and ideals Of the Great Nation and make the land good once again

Table of Content

Table of Contents

I. On Reform Legislation

a. <u>Decl. of Indep. from HOA government — 2000</u>

At this time when advocates are urging homeowners to present reform bills to their legislature, this earlier post of mine revealed the problem dealing with the legislature from the very beginning. This 2014 repost refers to my appearance before the Arizona HOA Hearing committee in 2000, which also appeared in Robert Nelson's book (p. 102) published by the Urban Institute Press.

****

"In 2000, as a naïve and newbie to the politics at state legislatures, Arizona in particular, I addressed the HOA Study Committee on September 7th (3rd such meeting of unfulfilled 7) and submitted a statement titled, "HOMEOWNER'S DECLARATION O F INDEPENDENCE from homeowner association governments." In it I quoted parts of the Decl. of Indep. And informed the committee that I had hoped that these hearings would bring forth a list of grievances for which homeowners were seeking redress.

[In 2000 I testified – – -]

"And as in those times of 1776, a small, principled and dedicated group of citizens are seeking a redress of their grievances. They first looked to the existing government, the HOA Board, and failing to obtain satisfaction therein, must seek other means of redress – a radical change in the concept and legal structure of the homeowner association controlling document, the CC&Rs.

"Mr. Chairman, ladies and gentlemen of the Committee, at this time I had hoped that the citizens of Arizona would be able to present and enumerate their long list of abuses, and solutions to these abuses, similar to as is found enumerated in the Declaration of Independence, without the interference and obstruction by elements of these 'oppressive governments.' I see that this will not be the case.

"The people of Arizona only wish to be able to present their case before this Committee in a fair and just manner. However, sadly I feel that, because of the composition of the committee, the homeowners are actually being placed on trial; that they are being asked to justify their grievances before their oppressors" [CAI].

****

Today, I think it would be helpful to adopt my statement and add those grievances that you feel need to be solved, and submit the entire package to your legislature and the media. It would be your declaration from HOA governments, your petition for redress. Of course, the more signatures you have the better.

b. A united, national front to HOA reform legislation (2023)

A private Facebook group has undertaken a gallant and tedious effort to inform advocates across the country proposing reform legislation. Its Admin, Patrick, provides a list of numerous bills that are applicable to all states with modifications. Thus, I proposed a broad sweeping "intent section" by the homeowner rights advocates to be included in all proposed legislation under the Homeowner Reform Leaders National Group (HRLING). It should be added as the last section to all bills, e.g., "Section2. Intention of . . . HRLNG."

As for specific legislation I proposed, I make reference to the "Homeowner Association Consent to be Governed Agreement An Act (to be known as the 'Truth in HOAs' Act," paragraphs 1 and 4, March 2011).

1. "No provision of any contract or any declaration of covenants, conditions, and restrictions affecting lawful property uses of residences in a subdivision or condominium is enforceable in this state unless the party seeking to enforce the provision proves by clear and convincing evidence that 1) the provision being enforced was knowingly and voluntarily agreed to by all parties against whom it is being enforced; or 2) all parties against whom the provision is being enforced knowingly and voluntarily agreed to be bound by the provision without reading or understanding it.

2. "Therefore, the CC&Rs or Declaration for any planned community, condominium association or homeowners association shall state that, 'The association hereby waivers and surrenders any rights or claims it may have, and herewith unconditionally and irrevocably agrees to be bound by the US and State Constitutions and laws of the State as if it were a local public government entity.'"

c. Two distinct levels for HOA legislation (2019)

I have classified two levels of HOA reform legislation that are needed to bring justice to homeowners: systemic and operational.

By "systemic" I mean inherent in the structure and legal model of HOA governance, which involves constitutional issues concerning the validity of the declarations and the pro-HOA state laws. The controversy focuses on the defenses of the HOA legal scheme, such as, private contract interference and "agreement to be bound." The contractual defense denies the application of the Constitution and the surrender and waiver of any rights that members claim to be denied. The agreement defense says the private contract was valid and legally agreed to by the home buyer, even though *contract law 101* is usurped by the equitable servitudes doctrine.

By "operational" I am referring to the management and operation of the day-to-day HOA that is regulated by existing pro-HOA laws and the adhesion CC&Rs. Reforms at this level are, for the most part, attempts to restore rights and privileges denied by the constitutional defenses mention in the above paragraph. This defense focuses on *the law is the law* and any concerns for fair, just and equitable treatment are not addressed in any of the states or governing documents, and therefor are irrelevant.

The purposes and aims in the Declaration have no bearing on the purposes and aims found in the Preamble to the Constitution.

It should be obvious that the operational reforms are limited by the existing failure to achieve constitutional reforms. Addressing the broader constitutional issues will greatly help the operational problems that concern most homeowners.

d. Analysis of The Homes Association Handbook (2006)

(Urban Land Institute Technical Bulletin #50 (1964))

The reader of this publication cannot but come away with the distinct realization that the authors promoted certain aspects of planned communities while deliberately avoiding a solid presentation of a number of serious concerns. It is a comprehensive manual, except for any discussion of the form of democratic governance of the community, for the mass merchandising of a profit-making business enterprise. Not only does this 422 page publication promote the selling of planned communities to the public, the federal government agencies, local governments, the mortgage companies and to the Realtors, it provides sample Declarations, Articles of Incorporation and Bylaws for use by the attorneys for developers(1). This use of sample forms(2) (similar to the legal forms that can be found in any legal research library) serve as guidelines and is a common practice used by the attorneys, which explains the commonality of many of the most oppressive and harsh terms and conditions imposed on homebuyers.

Yet, the word "democracy" is mentioned only a handful of times, and in the context of democratic form of leadership as with,

The other [as opposed to a bureaucratic style of leadership] requires more participation in order to give members a feeling of satisfaction with association operations; it may be called the 'democratic style'. (3) [emphasis added].

And, when the Handbook addresses specific covenants for inclusion in the Declaration for the developer turnover of the association to the homeowners,

It is our conclusion, however, that generally it is unwise to plan for the selection of the management of a homes association by something less than a fully democratic process (See Chapter 15).

However, Chapter 15, "Creating the Association and its Facilities", simply deals with a variety of non-governing topics, and includes marketing techniques as well as weighted voting in favor of the developer and benevolent paternalism by the developer controlled board.

Another example of the complete disregard for the constitutional and property rights of the homebuyers are the guidelines for handling the priority of liens that the authors felt was needed to protect the interests of the developer and the mortgagor, and to insure the continued existence of the corporate entity proposed to manage the planned community, the "automatic homes association"(4) . While this Handbook recognizes the problem with the timing of when the covenants running with the land become binding, at the time the developer sells the first lot, it advises that the states will protect the HOA from any homestead exemption because of this priority of liens(5), but urges the need to insert wording to grant the mortgagor a priority lien before this "developer" lien(6). The home-buying public protections, as was the intention of the various state legislatures when creating the homestead protection, was intentional disregarded by the advertising of this technical oversight.

Over the 42 years since the publication of The Homes Association Handbook, it has become the "bible" for the mass merchandising of planned communities with the accompanying affect on American society, its values and the loss of individual property rights, and the loss of fundamental rights and freedoms upon which this country was founded. The Handbook was supported by several federal agencies and real estate interests(7), and continues to be supported by these same entities along with state legislatures and local municipalities, with the same apparent disdain for the protection of American liberties and freedoms.

The mantra of "less government intervention", this call for a laissez-faire policy by reputable libertarian public interest firms, masks the prevalent protectionism of planned communities by the states and their failure to protect a segment of society from the predator marketing tactics of the real estate industry.

Notes

1. Appendices F, G, H.
2. Appendices K, L.
3. In Chapter 16, Leadership Style, Skill and Sources, § 16.2, Bureaucratic of Democratic? It May Depend on Common Facilities
4. Term used for today's mandatory membership association.
5. "We believe that the lien of assessments will, in all states, be recognized as superior to and unaffected by the homestead exemption". P. 322.
6. "In absence of an express provision altering priorities, the court held that the lien of the assessments was superior to the lien of the mortgagor . . . a suggested provision dealing with priorities may be found in Appendix F." p. 321.
7. From the cover page: the Federal Housing Administration, US Public Health Service, Office of Civil Defense, Urban Renewal Administration, Veterans Administration, and the National Association of Home Builders. The Urban Land Institute was formed in 1936 as a research division of the National Association of Real Estate Boards (now the

National Association of Realtors) under the name of the National Real Estate Foundation (see generally, Community Associations: The Emergence and Acceptance of a Quiet Innovation in Housing, Donald R. Stabile (Greenwood Press 2000).

e. <u>America's homeland: HOA law vs. Home rule law (2022)</u>

Why are there private HOA governments when there are home rule, charter governments?

Getting down to the issues of state laws relating to local governments, let's examine the doctrine of home rule. Under the home rule doctrine local communities are permitted a large degree of independence even to the extent that state legislative action is not necessary. What is home rule? In simple terms, it is a grant of authority and power — of independence — from the legislature to local communities. (See HOAs violate local home rule doctrine and are outlaw governments; AZ Supreme Court, *Tucson v. Arizona*, CV-11-0150-PR (2011).)

All the states have a version of home rule that varies in the degree of independence granted to a local governments and under what terms. Check your state laws under home rule or charter government. Strict states treat the home rule powers strictly as set forth in the statutes, like agency enabling acts. Most states have allowed for wider freedoms to local home rule governments, with some allowing for local government charters functioning as a local constitutions. In all cases it's a grant of independent governance from the legislature on local matters.

As an example, Arizona's Constitution allows for home rule charter governments.

"The purpose of the home rule charter provision of the Constitution was to render the cities adopting such charter provisions as nearly independent of state legislation as was possible. . . . '[A] home rule city deriving its powers from the Constitution is independent of the state Legislature as to all subjects of strictly local municipal Concern.'"

The masquerade

Given this existing legal mechanism for strong, independent **local control**, why was there a need for the creation and approval of, and the support for, private government HOAs? Could it be as Prof. McKenzie stated in his 1994 book, *Privatopia? "CIDs [HOAs/POAs/RCAs] currently engage in many activities that would be prohibited if they were viewed by the courts as the equivalent to local governments."*

It's obvious that it was not to create healthy, productive communities. Was it a business venture from the start to make profits for the originators masquerading as a public serve and benefit?? Was it for the real estate agents and the home builders, and to cut state government costs?

HOA associations are political bodies

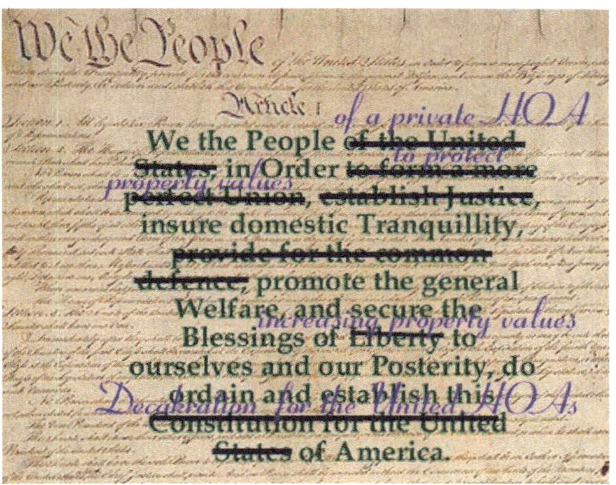

The effective management of a political community, as are HOAs, and remain part of the greater political communities of their state and federal government, necessitates a rejection of the HOA legal scheme and its protectives laws. There are no legitimate reasons why HOA governed communities cannot exercise effective and productive self-government while being subject to constitutional law under home rule statutes.

Home rule doctrine existed long before the advent of the HOA legal structure in 1964. That is not to say that it would have solved all problems and be a perfect government, but it would be a government under the Constitution, part of the Union, like all other forms of local government.

If the initial 1964 HOA concept had included home rule provisions, then there would be no need for a restructuring.

f. Preface to HOA Common Sense (2021)

The title of this pamphlet, "Common Sense," was chosen to identify and relate to the aims and purposes of the original 1776 pamphlet by Thomas Paine, Common Sense. Prior to the American Revolution it was Paine who provided the reasons and justifications for overthrowing the oppression government of King George III. He raised the consciousness of the colonists as to their second-class citizenship with respect to the British Empire, and something had to be done about. It was widely read by the Founding Fathers who did do something about it.

With a similar object in regard to oppressive, authoritarian HOA regimes, I present a summary of the essential issues that must be similarly remedied to bring about substantive changes to planned community/condo private governance.

Clarifications of meanings and concepts

A nation consists of a distinct population of people that are bound together by a common culture, history, and tradition who are typically concentrated within a specific geographic region. The common, binding element of HOAs is its organic law foundation, from which flow all state laws and the declarations of CC&Rs boilerplate, is based on The Homes Association Handbook of 1964.

An HOA is the governing body of a condominium or planned unit development (PUD) functioning for all intents and purposes as a de facto local political community government, but not recognized as such by state governments.

An organic law is a law, or system of laws, that form the foundation of a government, corporation or any other organization's body of rules. A constitution is a particular form of organic law for a sovereign state. The US has indeed a set of documents constituting its organic law.

Definition of HOA-LAND: HOA-Land is a collection of fragmented independent principalities within America, known in general as "HOAs," that are separate local private governments not subject to the constitution, and that collectively constitute a nation within the United States.

Read the book: HOA Common Sense: rejecting private government, a summary of 6 constitutional defects.

g. HOA Common Sense, No. 1: The New America of HOA-Land (2013)

This Commentary is the first in a series on the topic of HOA Common Sense. The political and social changes in our society brought about by the adoption and acceptance of the HOA legal scheme has created a new America of authoritarian, private governments known as HOAs. They function as independent principalities. The values, beliefs, principles, ethics, and morality of today's America would shock the Founding Fathers.

In 2008 I wrote, "Historians have referred to the American Revolution as the 'American Experiment'" and

> "The birth of the Second American Experiment went largely unnoticed. Under an unspoken alliance, the public was not informed of this experiment in the privatization of government. . . . This second experiment was not a strengthening of democracy, but one that promoted and established – with the support and cooperation of the state legislatures – private, contractual, authoritarian, government regimes. (Homeowners Associations: the Second American Experiment.)"

Earlier, in the 2007 paper, The Fall of the American Experiment:* Homeowner preference for HOA regimes, it was argued that,

> "As with the Articles of Confederation, the HOA Declaration must be scraped and replaced with a new "constitution," a municipal charter that allows for local individual ordinances and access to community amenities based on a community taxing district model, but subject to the same obligations, restrictions and laws as are our municipal entities. This approach would indeed retain the subdivision planned community real estate "package", and would

be a much-improved model of local autonomy, of local home-rule, still within the framework of the Constitution and laws of the land."

The people of America must escape the dogmas of today that have brought about a dysfunctional federal government and dysfunctional state legislatures that have renounced the Constitution. State governments have permitted the HOA principalities to function and govern the people independent of the Constitution. What purpose, then, does our Constitution serve?

These HOA governments are also dysfunctional and reflect our society. The people must replace these irrational dogmas with a sensible analysis of the current social and politic climate of America. A common sense approach by the people is needed to take a fresh look and what's wrong with America and what's wrong with the HOA legal scheme – for their children and their grandchildren.

h. Establishing the New America: the NJ Supreme Court opinion in the Twin Rivers HOA case (2008)

Last year, the NJ Supreme Court ruled on the free speech issues presented in a homeowners' suit against the Twin Rivers HOA[i]. This month, law professors Paula A. Franzese and Steven Siegel addressed the court's opinion in their joint Rutgers Law Journal article[ii] and their concerns regarding the legal constitutional status and public policy toward homeowners associations. Important legal doctrines, laws, arguments, issues and concepts are explored in this important article. This commentary presents certain issues raised by the authors in their article.

Citing the Court's opinion,

> "Our holding does not suggest, however, that residents of a homeowners association may never successfully seek constitutional redress against a governing association that unreasonably infringes their free speech rights.[iii]"

the authors argue

> "[T]he Court's resolution places it . . . providing a framework for a new constitutional approach to free speech in the context of homeowners associations, while also making clear that traditional private law concepts remain fully applicable to homeowners associations. . . . [T]he Court's opinion reveals that the Court did indeed announce the framework of a new constitutional approach to CICs [common interest communities] . . . .[iv]

> " The Court held that a homeowners association's regulations are not subject *exclusively* to the private law doctrines of contract and property. Rather, aggrieved residents may also seek constitutional redress. The *Twin Rivers* decision is not a model of clarity.[v]

> "[T]hat determination [the rejection of the Coalition case precedent] could be understood to mean that an aggrieved homeowner's sole remedy against an association's speech-infringing regulations lies *exclusively* in the private-law doctrines of contract and property.[vi]"

The New Jersey Coalition precedent spoke of a "historical path of free speech", moving from parks, squares, the "commons", to downtown business districts and shopping malls. The authors raise the issue, *"Similarly, in Twin Rivers, the relevant constitutional question was whether the 'historical path of free speech' has moved from public municipalities to private homeowners associations.*[vii] "

"Furthermore, the Court equated "residential" with inherently "private"- a determination made without explanation, and one that is inconsistent with the long held notion that streets held open to the public serve a vitally important function in connection with the rights of free expression and assembly.[viii]

> "[H]omeowners associations are the inheritors of the realm of open public discourse that once was exclusively undertaken in town halls and on public streets. Today, that discourse often occurs in private "community centers" and on streets that are open to the and maintained by the public with taxpayer dollars, yet nominally under the ownership of homeowners associations.[ix]"

The Court's opinion seems to adhere to the common law "standard reference", the

Restatement of Property, which supports the deference to private property law over constitutional law, "*The question whether a servitude unreasonably burdens a fundamental constitutional right is determined as a matter of property law, and not constitutional law*[x]." Here we have a definite statement that the US Constitution is not the supreme law of the land, that it shares authority with private property law advanced by the real estate special interest, and apparently agreed to by the NJ Supreme Court. **Welcome to New America!**

The authors feel that the constitutional question was not satisfactorily delineated.

> "[T]he Twin Rivers decision is unsatisfactory in many respects, because it lacks clarity and a firm underpinning in settled constitutional doctrine. The Court's failure to anchor its decision in established constitutional doctrine is particularly unfortunate, because there is substantial precedent available and adaptable to the homeowners association paradigm [legal concept or model].[xi"]

Furthermore, the authors also raise the question of the proper standard of judicial review. Simply stated, based on certain factors, the burden that the government must meet to restrict a constitutional right can be any legitimate government interest to a narrowly tailored and strictly defined government necessity that has no alternatives but to restrict the constitutional right. Which applies to private government HOA restrictions? It appears the Court rejected traditional constitutional doctrine for some vague new standard.

> "For example, under settled First Amendment doctrine, government regulation of speech in traditional public forums is **subject to heightened judicial scrutiny**. In that context, government may enforce such reasonable time, place, and manner restrictions only if the restrictions are content-neutral, are **narrowly tailored** to serve **a significant government interest** and leave open ample alternative channels of communication. [emphasis added].[xii]

> "The necessary implication is that the Court in Twin Rivers determined that homeowners associations play an important role in the civic life of New Jersey, and thereby **warrant a new standard a constitutional standard that reflects the special status of associations**. The Court left for another day the delineation of that standard. [emphasis added].[xiii]"

Now, no matter how one feels about homeowners associations, it cannot be argued that the acceptance and preference of homeowners associations by homebuyers, government officials, the courts, and by the various state legislatures is creating a **New America** inconsistent and contrary to the America of our Founding Fathers. For more reading on *Establishing the New America of independent HOA principalities* see PVTGOV.

Notes

[i] *Comm. for a Better Twin Rivers v. Twin Rivers Homeowners' Ass'n*, 929 A.2d 1060 (N.J. 2007).
[ii] *The Twin Rivers Case: Of Homeowners Associations, Free Speech Rights and Privatized Mini-Governments*, Paula A. Franzese and Steven Siegel, 5 RUTGERS J.L. & PUB. POL'Y 630 (2008). Part of the issue on *Homeowner Associations: Problems and Solutions***.**
[iii] Id., 743.
[iv] Id., 733.
[v] Id., 742.
[vi] Id., 746.
[vii] Id., 739.
[viii] Id., 744.
[ix] Id., 751.
[x] *Restatement Third, Property: Servitudes,* § 3.1 Validity of Servitudes: General Rule, comment h, p.359.
[xi] Supra n. 2, 750.
[xii] Supra n. 2, 748.
[xiii] Supra n. 2, 750.

i. <u>CAI firmly supports the New America of HOA-Land (2011)</u>

This issue of the Community Association Institute's house organ, Common Ground, has the strongest language for the triumph of private agreements to supersede the US Constitution, making the Constitution a meaningless piece of paper, a meaningless document, and an empty compact between the people and the state. "The right to regulate activities within a community association is an embodiment of our constitutional rights to enter into agreements with our neighbors" so proclaims CAI. It implies that the community association is just another corporate entity, and not the governing body that regulates and controls the people within its borders, which is the essential ingredient that distinguishes a corporation from a political government, a state.

CAI is falsely arguing that anybody can write an agreement to circumvent the Constitutional protections that forms the basis of our political system of government. In essence, CAI is advocating the rejection of the Constitution as the supreme law of the land and you and your neighbor can draft a new constitution as you see fit, ignoring the original Founding Fathers document. And so can another group, and another, and another, and so on. Why Is CAI arguing so? Perhaps because as private organizations, HOAs are not bound by the Constitution and can do as they please – the Constitution be damned!

CAI bitterly complains in this piece about one "disgruntled resident "[who] used the power of government to limit the freedoms of association residents" and caused Arizona to use its legitimate police powers to regulate people and organizations, and to protect the constitutional free speech rights to fly the Gadsden Flag in HOAs

And, seemingly desperate, CAI lets its readers know where it stands: The one constant is that your colleagues at CAI, working through 33 state legislative action committees, are fighting to protect associations and ensure a healthy business environment for the companies that support our communities" (Emphasis added). CAI does not stand for the people, but for the undemocratic governing body of subdivision territories known as homeowners associations. And, CAI says it loud and clear, making it quite explicit: CAI is "fighting to . . . ensure a healthy business environment for the companies that support our communities."That is, for their members, the lawyers and their self-proclaimed professional management firms. Let the Legislators hear well!

CAI is firmly behind the New America of HOA-Land of independent principalities unaccountable to any state in the Union. A balkanized hodge-podge of independent "city-states, under a parallel constitution known as the Uniform Common-Interest Ownership Model Act (UCIOA) and its variants across this country. Brought to you by the legal-academic aristocrats who have avoided any discussion of secession or repudiation of the principles of our American system of government. But, running to the state for protection as any principality must do. And the civil government of the state abdicates its duties under the US and state Constitutions, and protects these regimes against its own citizens.

Source: "Fees, Finances and Flags," Common Ground July-Aug 2011, CAI.

j. **Authoritarianism in America; authoritarianism in HOA-Land (2022)**

Some 23% of Americans live in HOA-Land, that collection of fragmented independent principalities known, in general, as HOAs. HOAs are separate, local private governments not subject to the constitution, and collectively constitute a nation within a defined geographical region known as the United States.

> *"A nation consists of a distinct population of people that are bound together by a common culture, history, and tradition who are typically concentrated within a specific geographic region."*

Jonathan Chait (Nymag.com, Jan. 3, 2022), wrote last week, ***"****You can't stop authoritarianism unless you understand it."* Consequently, my continued effort to reorient and reeducate HOA BODS and its followers.

The HOA is truly a totalitarian democracy. In 2019 I wrote, "Authoritarianism in the HOA-Land Nation"

> *"A totalitarian democracy . . . retains full power of . . . the right of control over everything and everyone. Maintenance of such power, in the absence of full support of the citizenry, requires the forceful suppression of any dissenting element except what the government purposely permits or organizes."*

The authoritarianism of HOA-Land is masked by a thorough indoctrination that the real estate subdivision is a democratic community because the members are allowed to vote, as meaningless as it is. It seems that the more predisposed to authoritarian control the more the member acts as a diehard, dogmatic, true-believer in the BOD.

Read more Cult behavior within HOA-Land.

k. **proposed HOA constitutionality bill (2021)**

Now is the time for all good homeowner advocate leaders
to come to the aid of member-owners

who are living in HOAs and suffering abuse, financial and emotional distress as a result of BODs being protected by Arizona laws. These abuses are easy to understand and support! (See HOA Common Sense: rejecting private government and The HOA-Land Nation Within America).

A quick and simple — but highly effective — bill that was proposed in March 2011 and will bring relief to homeowners being treated as second-class citizens by state laws in support of the HOA legal scheme. It was ignored by Arizona advocates and dismissed by the Legislature.

> "No provision of any contract or any declaration of covenants, conditions, and restrictions . . . is enforceable in this state unless the party seeking to enforce the provision proves by clear and convincing evidence that 1) the provision being enforced was knowingly and voluntarily agreed to by all parties . . . . Any representation or statement

> offered as clear and convincing evidence . . . shall include a signed statement containing the following, beginning with "I understand that I can ask that the following be read and explained to my satisfaction.
>
> "So reads an excerpt from my proposed "Truth in HOAs" statute that should be made law in each and every state. That is, if indeed the legislature stands by the Declaration of Independence and the US Constitution, which we are hearing so much about in the media nowadays."

The *"The Truth in HOAs Act,"* as I called it, allows each state to modify the proposal in accordance with its state HOA/condo acts — shown in square brackets []. Also, subsection (3) contains a list of acknowledgements that can be tailored to each state's advocate lobbying efforts. See Arizona Truth in HOAs statute . The essential bill section is contained in subparagraph (4).

> "Therefore, in reference to subsection 3(d) above, the CC&Rs or Declaration for any planned community, condominium association or homeowners association shall state that, "The association hereby waivers and surrenders any rights or claims it may have, and herewith unconditionally and irrevocably agrees to be bound by the US and State Constitutions and laws of the State as if it were a local public government entity."

The real estate subdivision or condominium will not be affected by requiring HOAs to join with other forms of local government and be subject to the Constitution as a home rule entity. See HOAs violate local home rule doctrine and are outlaw governments.

This 2022 legislative session offers a unique, one-time opportunity to get the message across and to educate the legislators. **Remaining silent on the issues only plays into the pro-HOA hands of CAI and offers excuses by the media not to cover HOA abuse.** Not only will you find "ammunition" in support of your arguments as contained in the 2 above publications, but also in my Arizona Supreme Court amicus brief filed and accepted in Tarter v. Bendt (note vi), in Can HOA members expect justice in Arizona courts?).

My arguments are summarized in the Commentary. As is my approach, my arguments are supported by legal authority and hard evidence documents, which CAI ignores, and YOU lose! They must be exposed if the legislators are to be fully informed on the reality of HOA-Land. As leaders who are internet publishers, **actions speak louder than words!**

1. **AZ bill, SB 1148, seeks to restore OAH adjudication of HOA disputes (2011)**

The Arizona bill, SB 1148, seeks to overcome the objections of the appellate court in Gelb, and restore due process protections to homeowners in HOAs by means of OAH adjudication. (See Advocate submits amicus brief in AZ supreme court appeal of HOA due process).

Below is the explicit statement of intent for this legislation, of which one purpose is to protect the consumer who buys a home in an HOA.

Sec. 4. Legislative findings and intent; department of fire, building and life safety; community disputes

It is the intent of the legislature to find, determine and clarify all of the following after careful consideration of the case Gelb v. Department of Fire, Building and Life Safety, 1 CA CV 09-0744, filed October 28, 2010 (Ct. App. 2010):

1. The department of fire, building and life safety has exercised substantial responsibility for many years in the enforcement and application of state laws and private contracts that regulate the relationships between those who reside in and those who control certain types of common housing, namely, mobile home park residential communities.

2. The legislature has determined that while the direct licensure of mobile home parks and their owners may not have been necessary, the regulation of their private, legal relationships with their tenants has been and continues to be an important consumer protection function of the department of fire, building and life safety and that department has developed considerable expertise in interpreting, enforcing and applying the statutes relating to these mobile home communities and in interpreting, applying and enforcing the terms of the leases, rules and other documents that regulate the relationship between

the residents of the mobile home parks and the owners and managers of those parks, and doing so in a cost-effective manner for the residents.

3. The legislature further determines and finds that while direct licensure and regulation of condominiums and planned communities may not be necessary at this time, the legislature has repeatedly found over the years that owners in condominiums and planned communities are frequently subjected to inconsistent, unreasonable and often unlawful enforcement and application of the declarations, rules and bylaws that govern their communities, their managers and their boards of directors, and owners are often unable to afford the cost of formally litigating their disputes in the superior court.

4. The legislature further finds that the continuing use of the existing hearing officer function in the department of fire, building and life safety will provide for an efficient use of already-established common interest community expertise at this agency, will provide an important consumer protection for owners in condominiums and planned communities and will efficiently and effectively provide for resolution of these common interest community disputes without the expense, formality and difficulty of requiring a trial in the superior court in every instance, and will do so without the cost and bureaucratic complexity of creating an entirely new administrative body to perform these important functions, while still maintaining the ability and right to recourse in the superior court, and without threat to the core functions of the judiciary.

m. <u>Arizona's new "Take That George!" law: officials don't have to defend HOA statutes (2010)</u>

This law was introduced, I firmly believe, as a result of my repeated chastising of our elected officials, over the past year, for their failure of to defend the constitutionality of the statutes that permitted the Office of Administrative Hearings (OAH) to adjudicate homeowner association disputes. I take it as a feeling of guilt that this bill was introduced.

The adjudication of HOA complaints by OAH had leveled the playing field somewhat, providing attainable —"affordable", to use a term used to defend the state's protection of HOAs — justice, where the homeowner could go before an independent tribunal, without a lawyer and without the need to know the 100 odd rules of civil procedure contained in some 200 pages of "legalize." The constitutionality of the statute was not defended by the Attorney General, or by the legislative leadership, resulting in a superior court disgraceful **default** decision. A homeowner has no place to go, not even to the OAH where he could once hope to have found justice. In the short history of OAH, pro per homeowners won 42% of their petitions against their HOA and its attorney.

This total disregard of my letter follows a flat denial, without explanation, of my February 11, 2009 Motion to Intervene, which was an abuse of discretion by Judge McMurdie. Perhaps it was because I had included the Attorney General's defense of the constitutionality of the statute in a prior case which would have caused a trial and an embarrassment to the AG), LC2007-00598 (Waugaman), given that the AG and Legislature now failed to defend the statute in this case. (See The State of Arizona will not protect buyers of HOA homes!, Feb. 29, 2009).

Ariz. Sess. L., Ch 105 (2010).
HB 2774 addition:
ARS 12-1841

> "D. This section shall not be construed to compel the attorney general, the speaker of the house of representatives or the president of the senate to intervene as a party in any proceeding or to permit them to be named as defendants in a proceeding. The attorney general, the speaker of the house of representatives or the president of the senate, in the party's discretion, may intervene as a party, may file briefs in the matter or may choose not to participate in a proceeding that is subject to the notice requirements of this section.

n. AZ Rep. explains failure of HOA reform legislation (2013)

I feel that my Footnote 1 from an upcoming commentary on **SB 1454** should stand by itself. Here's the paragraph and the Footnote.

> "Rep. Ugenti stated that each year there was *'a plethora of personal HOA legislation'* and

tried '*to spare the [committee] members the constant agony of many personal pieces of HOA legislation*,' as contrasted to the industry legislation.

"Footnote 1. I digress. My emphasis reflects, to a good extent, homeowners failing to see the broader picture beyond their HOA problem, such as raising substantive issues of constitutionality. Ugenti is saying that homeowners don't really understand the problems with HOAs, which only the HOA industry special interests can solve. It is evident that this is the view held by all state legislatures across the country. Homeowners have failed to deal with this reality."

A good part of this failure must be laid on the leaders of the homeowner rights advocacy movement. The leaders who appear, while paying lip service to constitutionality issues, to have failed to provide the necessary and adequate guidance and direction to accomplish HOA reform legislation. Instead, take for example the recent SB 1454 post and comments on the Privatopia Papers where portions of just one news article are quoted. The quotes indicate that the plaintiffs had "*done wrong to homeowners*" by winning their constitutionality challenge. The challenge was against certain actions taken by a rogue legislator with respect to an HOA bill. The balancing and explanatory parts of the article were not quoted.

Fred Pilot, a long term participant in HOA reform issues commented *about "So does this mean local governments can continue to utilize CID mandates?"*, which is totally irrelevant and nonapplicable to the victorious lawsuit. Or to his biased quote from the article. "*What has "CID mandates" got to do with the article*? And attempts to clarify the matter as to the implied, "*the plaintiffs have harmed the homeowners when they won*", resulted in their non-publication by the owner, Evan McKenzie.

Yet, McKenzie wrote that it was a fair question deserving an answer, but apparently not as a comment on Privatopia Papers. He wrote "*my understanding is that SB 1454 . . . prohibited municipalities and planning and zoning commissions from requiring developers to create HOAs.*" McKenzie lacks the understanding that these provisions were twice killed in this legislative session; and that Ugenti had to underhandedly get the bill passed in the wee hours of the morning on the last day of the session. But, I guess that has no bearing in this matter. It was only us evil plaintiffs who done homeowners in, under the principle that the end justifies the means.

Not a word about how this lawsuit sent a message to pro-HOA legislators and lobbyists that they can't get away with such flagrant abuse of the laws. Not a word. But the charges stand unanswered on the Privatopia Papers.

Unless the leaders get their act together, the arguments and implications of Ugenti's quote above will continue to dominate attempts at HOA reforms.

o. <u>The Florida HOA Battleground (HB 1397): police powers and the loss of fundamental rights (2009)</u>

This session must decide on Rep. Robaina's, the homeowner rights champion, omnibus or "all-inclusive" Community Associations reform bill, HB 1397, with its 190 pages of reforms. (The first 12 and a-half pages just summarize the changes). The bill attempts to deal with both the broader issues of the application of democratic principles and the use of police powers to regulate the acts and actions of HOA governance — requiring necessary actions while prohibiting others. State police power is often used to protect a weaker faction (segment or part of society) from a stronger faction.

HB 1397 jumps right into the application of Florida's police powers, permitted under the "establish justice", "insure domestic tranquility", and "promote the general welfare" objectives of the US Constitution. The bill begins with an addition of subsection (10) to § 20.165, Dept. of Business and Professional Regulation, that adds strong enforcement authority to employees of DBPR, such as to arrest, carry firearms, issue court subpoenas, etc. HB 1397 provides for very strong and very necessary enforcement authority if Florida laws are to have any meaning and standing as a bona fide law instead of a mockery of justice. There are also protections against home invasion by HOA officials and agents (§ 718.111(5)), paralleling that protection already provided to homeowners not living in HOAs by the 4th and 14th Amendments to the US Constitution. These reforms, alone, restore lost rights and freedoms enjoyed by non-HOA residents, and reduce the second-class citizenship of HOA residents. The New America of HOA-land special laws and "constitutions" protected by the state must cease! Rep. Robaina's bill goes a long way to restore the America of our Founding Fathers being quietly encroached by HOA-land special interests.

The second aspect to HOA reform legislation that concerns the systemic, the very structure of the legal scheme, failings and repudiations of American democracy. While the ends of the homeowner association mandatory governance of subdivisions are desirable in certain respects, the means to achieve these ends have been a disgraceful repudiation of the principles and values of the US Constitution with its concern for the protection of individual rights and freedoms. The very legal scheme or concept of homeowner associations flies in the face of the Constitution and has been defended by the weak argument of voluntary agreement to the loss of individual rights and freedoms by the simple argument, "Well, they still live there, don't they?"

There are questions of appropriate due process protections that only say "after notice and an opportunity to be heard" fines may be imposed by the board, without explicitly requiring an independent tribunal where witnesses and evidence can be question by the homeowner. And there are questions of "fair elections" procedures, of the need for free speech and access to all relevant information necessary to protect the homeowner from abusive actions by the board, of unusual punishment over miniscule unpaid assessments in terms of the greater loss suffered by foreclosure, where the HOA has not advanced any funds like the mortgage company (which is ascribing public government attributes to the private HOA entity), etc. How can a homeowner file fraud charges, as an example, when access to records is denied and not enforced by statute?

Analyzing a bill of the magnitude of HB 1397 places burdens upon the average homeowner with limited time and resources as opposed to the hired-hand, paid lobbyists of the special interest groups. Homeowners must understand that HB 1397 will be the result, for all practical matters, of a compromise between opposing parties, and the decision to support the bill must so accept this reality of governance. It will be a question of "pluses and minuses." Trade-offs will be made, but each must be weighed against the balancing scale of justice for the people, first and foremost. Rep. Robaina's bill is a must! Once passed into law, "blemishes" can be adjusted and will subject to the democratic process of give and take between the homeowners themselves, and between homeowners and the special interests

p. <u>Landmark FL HOA law imposes criminal conduct (2023)</u>

FL Session Law, Ch. 229 (2023), "Homeowners' Associations Bill of Rights," adds the following section imposing misdemeanor charges against certain violations for fraudulent elections.

> "FL § 720.3065. Fraudulent voting activities relating to association elections; penalties.—Each of the following acts is a fraudulent voting

> activity relating to association elections and constitutes a misdemeanor of the first degree, punishable as provided in s. 775.082 or s. 775.083"

This is a landmark bill that imposes criminal penalties on the conduct of the HOA and all persons involved in fraudulent HOA elections. Recent court decisions have held the private government HOAs are public entities with respect issues concerning the governance of the HOA.

Criticism of the board's conduct is subject to the constitutional protections of free speech. The Nevada Supreme Court opinion in Kosor ((*Kosor v. Olympia Companies,* NV No, 75669 (Dec. 31, 2020)) held that HOAs are public forums and referenced several California opinions serving as legal precedent.

> "[A] unit owner's association or a planned community association (association) may not prohibit a unit owner or member (member) from peacefully assembling and using private or common elements of the community . . . legitimate and valid criticisms of your HOA and its president and board are protected from HOA lawsuits of defamation and libel."

I find it incredible that there are homeowner rights advocates who find it difficult to see how challenges of constitutionality apply to private government HOAs. The 14th Amendment, Section 1, in part, "*No state shall make or enforce any law which shall abridge the privileges or immunities of citizens of the United States.*"

q. Colorado senator's guide to effective HOA legislation (2013)

An excellent guide for citizens seeking to effectively lobby their legislature to bring about desired change.

The author, Morgan Carroll, is an eight year Colorado legislator and is currently the Colorado Senate Majority Leader. Take Back Your Government sends a strong message to citizens to get involved in the legislative process if they sincerely seek change, otherwise the paid, special interest hired-hand lobbyists will strongly influence the legislators. And set the tone for new laws and changes to existing laws.

Carroll's opening chapter contains advice, such as,

"We elect people to represent our interests, but our elected

> representatives cannot adequately represent you unless they hear from you. . . . If you don't participate in your government, then the only remaining participants in the system are legislators and lobbyists."

And she reminds her readers that, "*Democracy only works when citizens participate, engage and become informed voters.*" And that is why democracy is a farce in the authoritarian HOA private governments where apathy abounds for numerous reasons.

Part II, Advocacy for Beginners, is chock full of "dos and don'ts" in contacting and dealing with bill sponsors, and how to draft and understand the wording and format of bills. The author provides advice for citizens such as, to "*suggest a solution,*" make your request "*shorter and simpler,*" and "*summarize prior attempts to fix the problem.*" Her concern for the people includes warnings that, "*every right [permitted by law] should come with a remedy or an enforcement mechanism, or it's an empty law.*" And there's the commonly found use of "shall" and "may," clarifying that "may" means "is permitted to" or "is authorized to," both of which mean making the act legal.

And there is much, much more about how to get heard, how to contact legislators, how to testify, creating fact sheets to support your position, etc. Definitely applicable, but not tailored just for HOA reforms. This book is a must read for advocates, especially HOA reform advocates who have faced a solid wall of indifference when seeking legislative change and who have been unsuccessful in the past.

Thank you Senator Carroll.

k. Support CO 22-1137 for HOA due process justice (2022)

Another HOA enlightenment bill has been proposed in Colorado, 22-1137, joining California's and Arizona's legislation to restore homeowner fundamental rights and freedoms. Reading the bill as introduced, it addresses a number of issues designed to provide meaningful due process, to good extent, allowing for small claims adjudication and restrictions, limitations on the HOA's right to fine, interest charges, late payments, work-out plan before foreclosure, and limits on the amount of collection to just 3 times amount owed (avoids unusual and cruel punishment charges).

What more can a homeowner ask for to obtain justice and fairness within the HOA government? **Go for the bill! Support it**! Get what you can before the evil empire strikes back and whittles the bill down! Yet, to my disappointment, a homeowner advocacy group has found problems with this bill, all relating to how it would cost the HOA more money.

What is needed, as I've repeatedly argued, is strong support for the sponsor, Rep. Naquetta Ricks, and an outpouring of emails to the legislators, especially to the committee members who will hear the bill. If there is a *Request To*

Speak option at the legislature, sign up and use it!

Related issues

In a broader view of HOAs as private, separate local governments keep in mind what has been ignored and bypassed by state legislatures across the country, including Colorado. Why are there private HOA governments when there are public home rule, charter governments?

All the states have a version of home rule that varies in the degree of independence granted to a local governments and under what terms. Given this existing legal mechanism for strong, independent **local control**, why was there a need for the creation and approval of, and the support for, private government HOAs?

(See America's homeland: HOA law vs. Home rule law; Colorado Constitution, Art. XX, §6, Home rule for cities and towns).

r. NC reform bills need your support (2023)

Three very material and important bills seeking meaningful HOA reforms are before the North Carolina General Assembly (legislature): H311, S312, and H542. (See 'There is no oversight' Proposed bills call for changes to HOAs in North Carolina). These bills address the two categories of reform legislation as I have defined them: constitutional and operational.

It has been my experience over some 23 years that reform legislation falls into two categorical levels: constitutional seeking to change the systemic HOA scheme, and operational seeking to apply the existing day-to-day laws and governing documents in a fair and just manner.

The average homeowner does not quite understand the broader constitutional issues but feels well the effects of the current day-to-day conditions. AN example of operational reform would be to change the time frame or approval percentage of an existing covenant. It's a procedural change.

H311,

An act to establish a community association oversight division in the office of the attorney general. In short, the AG is authorized to investigate HOA wrongdoing and to take remedial action including legal action, if so determined. The division is a rulemaking body — adopt and change rules — to carry out its authority. It is a constitutional 14th Amendment *due process* and *equal protection of the laws* bill.

S312,

An act that requires notice of liens and the ability to foreclose. A lengthy bill to inform the homeowner that a lien has been placed on his property and the right to work out a repayment plan. **While the right to foreclose is removed,** the HOA can proceed with legal action to obtain payment of the debt, like garnishment.

etc. It has a constitutional aspect in removing the right to foreclose – seen as a special law for a special entity, the HOA – and an operational aspect with respect to the procedures to follow in attempting to collect the unpaid assessments.

H542,

An act placing a limit on foreclosure and notice of a lien. The lien notice is similar to S312. The bill also sets a $2,500 minimum, or 1 year of unpaid assessments not paid within 30 days. It is an operational bill dealing with everyday procedures.

I prefer S312 over H542 since HOA foreclosure rights are unreasonable, against good public policy, and whose purpose is to serve as a punishment. What right does a private entity, that has not advanced any hard cash like a bank, have to receive foreclosure payments far in excess of the HOA assessment debt that also includes exorbitant attorney payments not found in the public sector?

s. North Carolina: second battleground for people's rights in HOAs (2013)

North Carolina is proud that it was the first state to vote for independence from Great Britain (Halifax Resolves, 1775). Today, some 238 years later, another battle for independence from oppressive government has commenced in the NC General Assembly. This time, it is the people subjected to authoritarian, oppressive private HOA governments who seek equal justice with regard to safeguarding their homes against HOA foreclosure. This time, it is the citizens of North Carolina who seek a redress of their grievances against the NC General Assembly that has supported, and continues to support, special laws for special groups.

> "In every stage of these oppressions, we have petitioned for redress in the most humble terms; our repeated petitions have only been answered by repeated injury." (Decl. of Indep.).

Today, the NC assembly has two HOA bills before it, HB 175 and HB 331: one seeks to impose harsher terms for HOA foreclosure rights, HB 331, and the other seeks to remove the unconscionable right of HOAs to foreclose, HB 175. While NC currently allows unconscionable nonjudicial foreclosure, HB 331 would now put the HOA in the same position of a Trustee holding a deed of trust with the "power of sale," which amounts to an auction sale without having to go to court. This amounts to putting the HOA in the same position not only as the mortgage holder, but as the trustee as well.

The bill further proscribes new foreclosure procedures that supersede the general NC foreclosure statutes, just for HOA foreclosures. There is nothing in the detailed procedures contained in 4 pages of the bill that addresses any procedures for the homeowner to contest the amount of debt being foreclosed by the HOA. What does the simple phrase, as used in the bill, "if not contested" mean?

On the other side of the battle-line, HB 175 does away with special foreclosure rights just for HOAs. And rightfully so! The right to foreclose has been argued on the basis of the need to collect assessments - read HOA "taxes" — so the HOA can survive. Well, this argument could apply to any nonprofit that seeks to foreclose in order to survive. But, there are no such laws protecting these nonprofits from failure, is there? And these nonprofit, charitable, and educational corporations can argue that they provide a public service, while the HOA provides services to a private group of people, only its members.

Other arguments against HOA foreclosure rights include:

- The HOA has not advanced any hard funds like a bank, yet it is treated as a public entity with the right to foreclose on the nonpayment of "taxes." But, the Assembly does not feel the need for checks and balances on the HOA board for this grant of special powers.

- The US Supreme Court has held that punitive damages, which the foreclosure essentially amounts to, in excess of 10 times the actual damages, violated the 8th amendment's prohibition on the infliction of cruel and unusual punishments. For example: Foreclosing on a $2,000 debt, of which $500 is the actual assessment debt, on a home valued at $140,000 amounts to a whopping 70 times the debt.

- Foreclosure discriminates and is essential an intimidation and punitive measure that is effective only on certain members and not others – only those who have paid their mortgage over the years so that the HOA can collect funds in excess of the existing mortgage. Is it fair for the good people who have paid and paid not only their mortgage but their HOA dues over the years to lose their home? I think not! But, on the other hand we hear their self-righteous chant that it's "unfair for others to pay for deadbeats" who are behind in their assessments. There seems to be a huge disconnect here.

I cannot entirely blame the members for this attitude, because they have been deceived. They have never been told the facts about the possible adverse financial conditions that could lead to holding them legally obligated for the debts of others. HOA membership is like buying into a small, privately held business that has limited ability to exit or to raise additional funds if needed. Also, the HOA is similar to a partnership where each member is jointly and severally obligated for the debts of the HOA.

If some members cannot meet their "fair share," any deficiency will be made up from those who can afford to pay. These additional funds, like now being needed by many HOAs, can only come from existing members, which can be imposed upon them through the courts.

Also, I cannot reconcile this obsession by members against letting the deadbeats get away with not paying their HOA debts that often amount to less than $2,000, but who say nothing when their HOA spends $5,000 – $100,000 in attorney fees pursuing trivial lawsuits against minor and questionable violations of rules. We see these cases in the media quite frequently. Something is wrong with the attitudes of members in HOAs, definitely wrong! The attitude of the HOA members themselves is discriminatory and unconscionable.

Which direction will the General Assembly take? For the people by ending the unconscionable and discriminatory HOA rights to foreclose, or for the defective HOA legal structure that denies homeowner protections?

t. CA bill AB 1410 – a step backwards for HOA homeowner rights (2022)

In 2018, California Civil Code §4515 was a major step in restoring fundamental protections for free speech by members with respect to HOA governing issues.

> "(a) It is the intent of the Legislature to ensure that members and residents of common interest developments have the ability to exercise their rights under law to peacefully assemble and freely communicate with one another and with others with respect to common interest development living or for social, political, or educational purposes."

Now, AB 1410 seeks to restrict these rights under the guise, it seems, that the HOA website is private and therefore it can adopt restrictive rules legally. In a typical "what you see is not what you get" maneuver, the bill would grant the HOA the power to moderate message content in strict opposition to legal holdings — that content based free speech is protected and any editing must be unbiased.

The bill sections start with §4515,

> *"(b) The governing documents, including bylaws and operating line 4 rules, shall not prohibit a member or resident of a common interest line 5 development from doing any of the following:"*

But watch out, what is granted is now removed under (b)(6) subparagraphs (B) and (C), and especially (D). In a "flip-flop," designed in my view to confuse the average homeowner, it then informs the homeowner that he is still protected because the HOA must follow the rules it is attempting to circumvent. (pp. 93-94).

What's the point? To make it difficult for homeowners to understand the legislation and their rights all well knowing that those in power will only cite the pro-HOA points and omit the pro-homeowner protections.

GOTCHA AGAIN! Don't fall for it!

This attempt by Rep. Rodriquez feels like an anti-slapp move if it were in the courts — an action to stifle free speech. Marjorie Murray presents 2 instances of where an anti-slapp motion can and should be used against the HOA. Contact Murray (info@calhomelaw.org) for more information.

Center for California HOA Law opposes the bill and urges Californians to contact their representatives and Judiciary Chair by phone. The committee will hear this bill this week.

u. Substantive SC HOA reform bill – end foreclosure (2019)

I've long argued for an HOA reform bill to address the serious ills of HOA foreclosure that I see as a punitive measure and constituting excessive and cruel punishment and a violation of the 8th Amendment.[1] SC's H 4741 pre-filled by Rep. Todd Rutherford. Surprisingly, it's has a long title that is very much *on point*.

> *A BILL TO AMEND SECTION 15-41-30, CODE OF LAWS OF SOUTH CAROLINA, 1976,* Relating to property exempt from attachment, levy, and sale, so as to provide that a debtor's interest in real property used as a primary residence may not be sold if the action was instituted by a homeowners association

attempting to collect unpaid dues, fees, or fines; to amend section 27-30-130, relating to the enforceability of a homeowners association's governing documents, so as to prohibit the enforceability of a provision granting a homeowners association the authority to foreclose on property; and by adding section 29-3-810 so as to prohibit a foreclosure action not authorized by statute.

For the HOA to collect any back dues there must be sufficient equity in the property over any mortgage. The HOA can only get $$$$ from long-time paying owners with little or no mortgage. Its overuse is purely a draconian punishment and feeding $$$$ for the HOA attorney! Municipal/state foreclosure doesn't involve substantial attorney fees that often exceed the debt owed the HOA, several times over. Shame on state legislatures that protect HOAs with special laws for special entities.

Isn't an HOA foreclosure also tantamount to an excessive fine?[2] It's a penalty for a violation of the CC&Rs. In *Timbs v. Indiana*[3] the US Supreme Court held, *"The Eighth Amendment's Excessive Fines Clause is an incorporated protection applicable to the States under the Fourteenth Amendment's Due Process Clause."* This opinion did not address the 8th Amendment's cruel and unusual punishment clause as also being applicable to the states under the 14th Amendment. However, the intent of the 14th Amendment was quite clear to the Supreme Court.

> "The Fourteenth Amendment's Due Process Clause incorporates and renders applicable to the States Bill of Rights protections "fundamental to our scheme of ordered liberty,"

This bill will no longer allow the owner's home to be treated as collateral for the survival of the HOA! The SCOTUS opinion should render HOA foreclosures null and void. It's up to the SC residents to make this bill become law! You must be proactive in supporting Rutherford.

References

[1] See "Draconian punishment and intimidation, No. 8," HOA Common Sense: rejecting private government, George K. Staropoli(2013).
[2] Technically speaking, the word "fine" means punishment order by the courts for a crime. A penalty is a punishment for breaking a law, or rule, or contract. In HOA-Land the terms or used quite loosely.
[3] *Timbs v. Indiana*, no. 17-1091 (U.S. 2019).

v. Effective HOA reform legislation (2023)

If advocates want truly effective legislative reforms, they must actively support their legislative champions sponsoring these reforms. There have been important successes as a result of the increased call for and proposed reform legislation in several FB social media groups.

However, these reforms MUST address the very broad and larger constitutional issues that deny homeowners rights — rights that people not living in HOAs enjoy. Simply stated, HOAs must be made part of the Union! The trickle-down effect would be enormous. All homeowners would be protected and treated fairly when their rights and privileges fall under the well understood laws of the land.

Here's a simple, straight-forward bill first proposed in March 2011 found in Proposed "consent to be governed" statute, the "Truth in HOAs" bill.

> "The CC&Rs or Declaration for any planned community, condominium association or homeowners association shall state that, 'The association hereby waives and surrenders any rights or claims it may have, and herewith unconditionally and irrevocably agrees to be bound by the US and State Constitutions and laws of the State as if it were a local public government entity.'"

Item 4 of the Truth in

w. HOA member Declaration of US and State citizenship (2015)

I am proposing that the following be urged as a bill in your state, which requires a mandatory statement of HOA member citizenship. (Revised August 1, 2015).

"Declaration of US and State citizenship

"With the understanding that the association, as a private entity and not a subdivision of the state, and as a de facto but unrecognized private government, is not subject to the restrictions and prohibitions of the Fourteenth Amendment to the US Constitution that otherwise protects the rights of the people against actions by public government entities;

"and that the governing documents in all legal practicality serve as the subdivision's constitution, taking precedence over state laws and over the state and US Constitutions unless specifically denied by any such laws or legal precedence;

"Therefore, the members of the association, having not waived or surrendered their rights, freedoms, privileges and immunities as citizens of the United States under Section 1 of the Fourteenth Amendment, and as citizens of the state within which they reside, the CC&Rs or Declaration for any planned community, condominium association or homeowners association shall state that, or be amended to comply,

'The association hereby waivers and surrenders any rights or claims it may have under law and herewith unconditionally and irrevocably agrees 1) to be bound by the US and State Constitutions, and laws of the State within which it is located, as if it were a subdivision of the state and a local public government entity, and 2) that constitutional law shall prevail as the supreme law of the land including over conflicting laws and legal doctrines of equitable servitudes.

'Furthermore, any governing documents of an association not in compliance with the above shall be deemed amended to be in compliance, and notwithstanding the provisions of any law to the contrary, a homeowners' association shall be deemed to have amended its governing documents to be in compliance.'"

II. On The Bill of Rights

a. Why is there a need for a Homeowners Bill of Rights? *(2007)*

As James Madison wrote in The Federalist No. 51, "If men were angels, no government would be necessary. If angels were to govern men, no internal or external controls on government would be necessary.

Preamble to the US Bill of Rights

"THE Conventions of a number of States, having at the time of adopting the Constitution, expressed a desire, in order to prevent misconstruction or abuse of its powers, that further declaratory and restrictive clauses should be added: And as extending the ground of public confidence in the Government, will best insure the beneficent ends of its institution:"

PVTGOV Proposed Homeowners Bill of Rights

1. The HOA is subject to the Fourteenth Amendment to the US Constitution as are all over government entities subject.
2. The HOA, and HOA directors, officers and committee chairs are subject to the municipality and state laws wherein the HOA resides.
3. No "ex post facto" amendments to the governing documents shall be permitted without the consent of all homeowners.
4. The taking of a homeowner's property rights by the HOA as a result of an amendment to the governing documents or rules and regulations, if

any, without a judicial order and without fair compensation is prohibited.

5. The HOA right to foreclose on a homeowner as a result of failure to pay any fines, penalties, costs or other charges not a bona fide assessment is prohibited.

6. Recognizing that the HOA does not stand in the same position as a mortgagor that has a substantial monetary investment in the home, or in the case of a mechanic's lien where the homeowner possesses greater powers over the mechanic, foreclosure shall not be permitted for amounts less than 80% of the fair market value of the home, with the balance of the sale proceeds belonging to the homeowner.

7. The directors, officers and committee chairs shall be residents and members of the HOA community.

Read Sen. McCain's comments on limited government and more on the purpose of a homeowner bill of rights

b. <u>The HOA legal scheme is ab initio unconstitutional *(2023)*</u>

TO: Legislative leaders in every state:

The HOA legal scheme based on the *Homes association Handbook* is ab initio unconstitutional.

In March 2006 I wrote Christopher Durso, editor of the Community Associations Institute's (CAI) monthly house organ, *Common Ground,* asking four questions in regard to the constitutionality of HOA's (CID, POA, planned unit development,

etc.) legal scheme. My concern was that <u>CC&Rs are a devise for de facto HOA governments to escape constitutional government</u> as presented in the 1964 "bible" that brought forth the legal scheme, *The Homes Association Handbook*.
Replacing democratic local governments with authoritarian private governments: Is this good public policy?

> *"Public policy today rejects constitutional government for HOAs allowing them to operate outside the law of the land. The policy makers have failed to understand that the HOA CC&Rs have crossed over the line between purely property restrictions to establishing unregulated and authoritarian private governments."*

Here are the four questions:

1. Is it proper for the state to create, permit, encourage, support or defend a form of local government of a community of people, whether that form of government is established as a municipal corporation or as a private organization that is not compatible with our American system of government?

2. Is it proper for the state to permit the existence of private quasi-governments with contractual "constitutions" that regulate and control the behavior of citizens without the same due process and equal protection clauses of the 14th Amendment; that do not conform to the state's municipal charter or incorporation requirements; or do not provide for the same compliance with the state's Constitution, statutes or

administrative code as required by public local government entities?

3. When did "whatever the people privately contract" dominate the protections of the US Constitution? The New Jersey Appeals Court didn't think so (*CBTR v. Twin Rivers*, 2006). Does "constructive notice," the "nailing to the wall," the medieval method of notice, measure to the requisite level of notice and informed consent to permit the loss of Constitutional protections?

4. Please state what, if any, are the government's interests in supporting HOAs that deny the people their constitutional rights?

Please respond to these fundamental questions of HOA constitutionality.

c. co-opting the HOA "homeowners bill of rights" *(2011)*

In 2008 the 1994 **UCIOA (Uniform Common Interest Ownership Act)** was modified to accommodate the outcry from homeowner rights advocates. This shortened version is known as the **Uniform Common Interest Ownership Bill of Rights Act** (UCIOBORA), and is a political maneuver to co-opt the real meaning and intent of a "bill of rights." Here's an explanatory excerpt from UCIOBORA:

> "Further, ULC [Uniform Law Commissioners] acknowledges that it will often not be feasible to enact UCIOA 3.0, in part because of the difficulty drafters in the States may encounter in integrating any new

> adoption of the existing Uniform Acts with the laws that may already exist in a particular state. For these reasons, ULC promulgated a free-standing and relatively short Uniform Act that addresses all of the 'association versus unit owner' issues touched on during the drafting of the 2008 UCIOA amendments. The free-standing Act is known as the Uniform Common Interest Owners Bill Of Rights Act or "UCIOBORA". While not all sections of UCIOBORA are identical to UCIOA 3.0, the concepts underlying each Act are the same, and are adjusted simply to recognize the simplified nature of UCIOBORA."

In short, UCIOA wasn't selling. It seems that UCIOBORA is the sad result of the political motives to get UCIOA selling again. It's a document that does not at all read like the US *Bill of Rights*, or any state constitution's Declaration of Rights (state constitution equivalent of the Bill of Rights), or even the *Declaration of the Rights of Man and Citizen* (France, 1793). Far from it. Rather it reads like your current CC&Rs and UCIOA with a number of concessions to reality. However, it lacks substantive protections of homeowner rights, such as: a fair and just due process by means of an independent tribunal; fair elections procedures with equal and fair access to membership lists, and equal opportunity appearances in the HOA newsletter/website; restrictions on the right to foreclose, since the HOA is not in the same position as a lender who had advanced hard cash; and enforcement by means of penalties against board violations of the governing documents, otherwise all such laws are just recommendations dependent on the goodwill of the affected persons.

A homeowners bill of rights is necessary because the Constitution with its Bill of Rights amendments does not apply to private HOA governments. HOA governments operate outside the Constitution, which is greatly desired and defended by HOA supporters as they would not be able to act in ways that a civil government cannot act. A statement in a declaration that says that the HOA is subject to the Constitution is meaningless, since the Constitution does not apply to private entities. What is necessary is a statement that the HOA acknowledges the Constitution as the supreme law of the land and irrevocably agrees to be subject to it as if it were indeed a government entity

Short History

In 1997, Elizabeth McMahon of AHRC filed a *Homeowners Bill of Rights* with the California Law Review Commission looking into revising California's HOA statutes. In 2000, George K. Staropoli submitted a statement to the Arizona Interim HOA Committee, *Homeowner's Declaration of Independence* from the HOA system of government. In 2006, AARP produced a public policy statement, *A Bill of Rights for Homeowners in Associations*, written by Houston attorney David Kahne. In 2006 the legal-academic aristocrats (lawyers for the real estate interests) at a Texas senate hearing proposed a Texas Uniform Planned Community Act (TUPCA). Responding to Texas homeowner rights advocates, the committee was told that UCIOA (the model act for TUPCA) was being modified to include a bill of rights section. In 2008, George K. Staropoli informed the California Law Review Commission of a proper *Members Bill of Rights* section to the Davis-Stirling Act (This section was later dropped from the revision).

d. **<u>Will ULC pursue HOA Member Bill of Rights? *(2020)*</u>**

> *"Can private parties enter into contractual arrangements, using adhesion contracts and a constructive notice consent, that serve to regulate and control the people within a territory (an HOA), to circumvent the application of the Constitution?"[1]*

In August I commented that I was working with 2 institutions on a Member Bill of Rights.[2]

> *"Currently, I am working with two leading institutions concerned with state laws and the constitutionality of the HOA legal structure. Addressing the Bill of Rights issue is relevant to conducting necessary research and studies. A Homeowners Bill of Rights would be a major step toward the equal protection of the laws for members of HOAs.*
>
> *"As a result of my proposed research by independent, objective researchers, the law will be clarified and all parties set straight as to their rights, and on the legitimacy and validity of independent private governments in America."*

The Uniform Law Commission (ULC) will decide on the 29th whether or not to undertake a study of my proposal for meaningful revision to its UCIOBORA (2008). It's composed of only attorneys appointed by state legislators and are pro bono. I must call to your attention the long established presence of CAI at ULC and with respect to UCIOA.

I believe that ULC will move ahead and make the Constitution and state laws living documents reflecting the overwhelming evidence for the need to admit that HOAs are invalid ab initio — from the very start — agreements and are unconstitutional.

Notes
[1] The "end of denial" of unconstitutional HOAs, August 5, 2020.
[2] HOA Bill of Rights redux, August 29, 2020. Updated, HOA bill of rights history updated Sept. 13, 2020

e. HOA bill of rights history updated (2020)

A brief history[i]
It should be noted when reading this brief history that in 1992 Community Associations Institute (CAI) modified its tax-exempt status from education (501(c)3) to a business trade entity (501(c)6) with increased lobbying rights.[ii]

Prior to 2000

In 1992, Roger Dilger wrote,

> *"For example, most of those who advocate the formation of RCAs HOAs]*

assume that RCAs . . . incorporate all the rights and privileges embodied in the US Constitution, including . . . the rights of due process and equal protection under the law found in the Fourteenth Amendment;[iii]*"*

In 1994 Evan McKenzie said it plainly, and is true today,

T]he property rights of the developer, and later the board of directors, swallow up the rights of the people, and public government is left as a bystander. . . . [Consequently,] this often leads to people becoming angry at board meetings claiming that their 'rights' have been violated – rights that they wrongly believe they have in a [HOA]. (p. 148).[iv]

Editors Barton and Silverman published *Common Interest Communities* in 1994, a report on 12 early HOA (CID) research studies addressing the debate between HOAs as private governments in relation to public government.[v] Their conclusions in regard to the environment and culture of HOAs included:

"Our research shows the tension created by combining neighboring and political social relations into this form of organization [common interest homeowner's association].

"This means that the association's objectives can only be decided on through [sic] discussions among the homeowners. As a result, the homeowners' association needs to meet

the basic democratic standards of openness, fairness, and representativeness to its members.

"The model of the informed consumer choosing the mandatory homeowners' association and its detailed restrictions, the 'servitude regime', fails to describe reality.

"[T]hey [certain homeowners] reacted with strong, negative emotions to apparent infringements on their own rights as private property owners. These residents treated the governing bard of directors not as trustees of the public interest but as neighbors who had unfair powers over them.
Our findings pf pervasive conflict and fear of conflict, accompanied by apathy and avoidance within the community, run counter to the normal picture of community organization."

Steven Siegel wrote in 1998,

"Many RCAs exercise powers traditionally associated with local government. . . . Although the traditional view of RCAs is that each homeowner consents to the regime or chooses to reside elsewhere, Siegel rejects this view and suggests instead that RCAs are the product of forces other than consumer choice, including local government land use policies and fiscal pressure on local governments leading to the privatization of local government services. Because of

the traditional view, RCAs rarely have been deemed state actors subject to the requirements of the Constitution. As private entities, RCAs regulate behavior in a way that is anathema to traditional constitutional strictures.[vi]*"*

As early as 1999 homeowner advocates, the late Lois Pratt and Samuel Pratt, made their case for a homeowner bill of rights, writing,[vii]

"The association shall exercise its powers and discharge its functions in a manner that protects and furthers the health, safety and general welfare of the residents of the community'[citing NJ law]. . . . In essence, this is the standard that defines the fundamental right of homeowners and the obligation of those in power. Every action of an association must conform to the standard: Does it promote the welfare and protect the rights of the members of the association?

"While the topic of 'Homeowner Rights and Responsibilities' is frequently presented for discussion – in books, articles, and conferences on RCA management and operations, in state laws, in association by-laws, and in board minutes – the focus of attention consistently turns to the obligations of homeowners, and scant attention is given to homeowners' rights. To date we have found no document that presents a thorough treatment of homeowner rights."

2000 and later

In 2000, before the Arizona Legislature's HOA hearing committee I made an appeal for a member bill of rights:

> *[Homeowner rights advocates] first looked to the existing government, the HOA Board, and having failed to obtain satisfaction therein, must seek other means of redress – a radical change in the concept and legal structure of the homeowner association and its controlling document, the CC&Rs. What is needed is an inclusion of a homeowners Bill of Rights and the removal of such onerous provisions that make the homeowner nothing more than an indentured servant, living at the suffrage of the board – pleased if the board is benevolent; living in fear if the board is oppressive.*[viii]

In 2005, some 5 years after my introductory statement to the Arizona Legislature, HOA member rights — an HOA Bill of Rights, a constitutional issue — took hold. Nothing developed until The California Law Review Committee (CLRC), in 2005, timidly announced a "Chapter 2, Members Rights, Article 1, Bill of Rights," in its preliminary draft to revising the applicable Davis-Stirling Act. It immediately disappeared from the initial draft of revisions, but upon repeated exchanges on homeowner rights by the late Mrs. Elizabeth McMahon and Donnie Vanitzian, and yours truly,

CLRC finally responded in 2005: "CLRC responded with, '*However, a bill of rights would probably go beyond the substantive rights that are currently provided in the law*' (MM05-03)," and,

> *"George Staropoli objects [2008] to the lack of any substantive extension of homeowner rights. In particular he objects to the lack of any provision addressing the relationship of CID law to the state and federal constitutions. See Exhibit p. 1. As indicated at Exhibit p. 2, Mr. Staropoli first raised these issues in 2005 and was informed at that time that they were beyond the scope of the recodification project. (First Supplement to Memorandum 2008-12)."*

In July 2006 AARP released its *A Bill Of Rights For Homeowners In Associations: Basic Principles of Consumer Protection and Sample Model Statute,* authored by Texas attorney, David A. Kahne.[ix]

Furthermore in 2006, *CAI's Tom Skiba thinks Staropoli's logic is flawed. 'The fact is that by statute, common law, contract, and decades of practice, community associations are not-for-profit entities,' Skiba says, 'and are and should be subject to the relevant and applicable business law, contract law, and specific community association or common-interest-development law in each state.'*[x]

In 2007 I urged the need for an HOA Bill of Rights, citing the intents and purposes of *The Preamble to the US Bill of Rights*:[xi]

"THE Conventions of a number of States, having at the time of adopting the Constitution, expressed a desire, in order to prevent misconstruction or abuse of its powers, that further declaratory and restrictive clauses should be added: And as extending the ground of public confidence in the Government, will best insure the beneficent ends of its institution:"

In 2007 a currently active CAI member and former President had this to say, "Thus, the question of whether a particular covenant in a contractually-created community violates an owner's constitutional rights of expression finds its answer in well-established property law jurisprudence."

In 2008, after a few years drafting, the Uniform Law Commission produced it bill of rights, ***Uniform Common Interest Bill of Rights Act*** **(UCIOBORA)** as a result of pressures frcm homeowner rights advocates, AARP, and others to provide homeowners with a bill of rights. It stated:

"The Need for a Free-Standing Home Owner Bill of Rights. . . . The reason is that each of these complex Acts has its detractors who have historically blocked adoption of these Acts in any state. . . . [And] of the difficulty drafters in the States may encounter in integrating any new adoption of the existing Uniform Acts with the laws that may already exist in a particular state. For these

reasons, ULC promulgated a free-standing and relatively short Uniform Act that addresses all of the 'association versus unit owner' [hints at similarity of 'management vs employees'] issues touched on during the drafting of the 2008 UCIOA amendments.[xiii]"

Tom Skiba, again in an unbelievable 2008 doubletalk statement declared:

"Community associations are not governments — many years of legislation and court rulings have established that fact beyond a reasonable doubt. Yet they are clearly democratic in their operations, electing their leadership from among the homeowners on a periodic basis. . . . The solution to that problem is not to replace democracy with tyranny, royalty, or some other form of government, but to work to make the democratic process better and to hold those elected accountable.[xiv]"

In 2008 Paula Franzese and Steven Siegel wrote with respect to the NJ Supreme Court opinion in Twin Rivers,

"The laissez-fare approach to CIC regulation is reflected in the statutory law, which affords exceedingly few rights and protections to homeowners association residents.[xv]*"*

In 2015 Deborah Goonan appealed to homeowners to write their Congressmen about the injustices in HOA-Land.[xvi] Her sample letter included,
"We have become a nation obsessed with property values to the exclusion of traditional American values," and

> *"Governance of HOAs is not currently required to be bound by Constitutional law, thereby resulting in a nation where 67 million people are not subject to equal protection under the law. In HOAs, The Bill of Rights Need Not Apply. The resulting inequality contributes to abusive governance, frequent conflict and abuse of the legal system."*

Goonan again in 2020, referencing Arizona's SB 1412 (held in Rules due to COVID-19 premature session closing) and addressing Florida's SB 623 (having since failed) wrote,

> *"It's a 52-page bill that, among other things, seeks equal protection of Constitutional rights for all residents of HOA-governed communities. . . The Bill of Rights would apply to all Florida HOA-governed communities."*[xvii]

The 2008 Uniform Law Commission's HOA bill of rights, UCIOBORA, is a document that does not at all read like the US *Bill of Rights*, or any state constitution's Declaration of Rights (state constitution equivalent of the Bill of Rights), or even the *Declaration of the Rights of Man and Citizen* (France, 1793). Far from it. Rather it reads like your current CC&Rs and the basic UCIOA with just a number of concessions to reality"[xviii].

The spirit of the *US Bill of Rights* must be made to prevail over the HOA-Land Nation.

NOTES

[i] Adapted from "HOA Bill of Rights redux," George K. Staropoli, *HOA Constitutional Government* (2020).

[ii] Evan McKenzie, supra n.1, pp. 115 -119; Donald R. Stabile, *Community Associations: The Emergence and Acceptance of a Quiet Innovation in Housing, p. 144* (2000). Funded by CAI and ULI.

[iii] Roger Jay Dilger, *Neighborhood Politics: Residential Community Associations in American Governance*, p. 160, New York Univ. Press (1992). Formerly WVU Prof. Political Science and Director of Political Affairs.

[iv] Evan McKenzie, supra n. 1.

[v] Stephen E. Barton & Carol J. Silverman, eds., *Common Interest Communities: Private Governments and the Public Interest*, Ch. 13, section, "Private Property and Public Life in the Common Interest Development," Institute of Government Studies Press, Univ. of Calif., Berkeley (1994).

[vi] Steven Siegel, "The Constitution and Private Government: Toward the Recognition of Constitutional Rights in Private Residential Communities Fifty years After Marsh v. Alabama," Wm & Mary Bill of Rights J., Vol. 6, Issue 2 (1998).

[vii] Lois Pratt and Samuel Pratt, A Bill Of Rights For Homeowners In Residential Community Associations (1999).

[viii] Homeowner's Declaration Of Independence, George K. Staropoli, statement to the Arizona HOA Interim Hearing Committee, Sept. 7, 2000.

[ix] [1] David A. Kahne "AARP HOA Bill of Rights," *AARP Public Policy Institute* (2006).

[x] "Call &Response," Christopher Durso, Ed., Common Ground — July - August 2006.

[xi] See "Why is there a need for a Homeowners Bill of Rights?," George K. Staropoli, *HOA Constitutional Government*.

[xii] "Former CAI president reaffirms property law superior to Constitution." (2007). Article on NJ Twin Rivers decision, 2007; Link to CAI blog not found Sept. 9, 2020.

[xiii] UCIOBORA, Prefatory Note, page 1.

[xiv] CAI CEO Skiba in his April 2, 2008 *Ungated* blog entry.

[xv] Paula A. Franzese and Steven Siegel, "The Twin Rivers Case: Of Homeowners Associations, Free Speech Rights And Privatized Mini-Governments", 5 RUTGERS J.L. & PUB. POL'Y 630 (2008).

[xvi] "Let's Get Some National Attention on HOA, Housing Issues," Deborah Goonan, Independent American Communities (2015).

[xvii] "Florida Legislature Considers HOA 'Equal Protection' Bill," Deborah Goonan, *Independent American Communities* (February 7, 2020).

[xviii] See "co-opting the HOA 'homeowners bill of rights.'", George K. Staropoli, *HOA Constitutional Government* (2011).

f. A California true HOA Bill of Rights (2017)

CA Chapter 236 (SB 407) (2017), just passed into law. A true Homeowner Bill of Rights. Thank you Senator Wieckowski. The bill in part,

The people of the State of California do enact as follows:

SECTION 1. Section 4515 is added to the Civil Code, to read:
(a) It is the intent of the Legislature to ensure that members and residents of common interest developments have the ability to exercise their rights under law to peacefully assemble and freely communicate with one another and with others with respect to common interest development living or for social, political, or educational purposes.

(b) The governing documents, including bylaws and operating rules, shall not prohibit a member or resident of a common interest development from doing any of the following:

(1) Peacefully assembling or meeting with members, residents, and their invitees or guests during reasonable hours and in a reasonable manner for purposes relating to common interest development living, association elections, legislation, election to public office, or the initiative, referendum, or recall processes.
(2) Inviting public officials, candidates for public office, or representatives of homeowner organizations to meet with members, residents, and their invitees or guests and speak on matters of public interest.
(3) Using the common area, including the community or recreation hall or clubhouse, or, with the consent of the member, the area of a separate interest, for an assembly or meeting described in paragraph (1) or (2) when that facility or separate interest is not otherwise in use.
(4) Canvassing and petitioning the members, the association board, and residents for the activities described in paragraphs (1) and (2)

at reasonable hours and in a reasonable manner.
(5) Distributing or circulating, without prior permission, information about common interest development living, association elections, legislation, election to public office, or the initiative, referendum, or recall processes, or other issues of concern to members and residents at reasonable hours and in a reasonable manner.

(c) A member or resident of a common interest development shall not be required to pay a fee, make a deposit, obtain liability insurance, or pay the premium or deductible on the association's insurance policy, in order to use a common area for the activities described in paragraphs (1), (2), and (3) of subdivision (b).

(d) A member or resident of a common interest development who is prevented by the association or its agents from engaging in any of the activities described in this section may bring a civil or small claims court action to enjoin the enforcement of a governing document, including a bylaw and operating rule, that violates this section. The court may assess a civil penalty of not more than five hundred dollars ($500) for each violation.

g. Calif. CLRC doesn't see need for HOA Bill of Rights *(2008)*

After several years of study, the California Law Review Commission, CLRC, has recommended a rewrite of the HOA/condo laws, the Davis-Striling Act, SB1921. While it has moved forward with this proposed rewrite, CLRC felt it not sufficiently important to also include a Member Bill of Rights (Chapter 2), and can add a bill of rights at some later time.

Read CLRC memorandum in regard to severe criticism of proceeding in an illogical manner, in a manner opposed to its constitutional obligations to protect the individual and private property rights of the people. It is an approach not followed in the adoption of our US Constitution.

"George Staropoli objects to the lack of any substantive extension of homeowner rights. In particular he objects to the lack of any provision addressing the relationship of CID law to the state and federal constitutions. See Exhibit p. 1. As indicated at Exhibit p. 2, Mr. Staropoli first raised these issues in 2005 and was informed at that time that they were beyond the scope of the recodification project."

Read more at . . .

h. AARP HOA Bill of Rights (2006)

David Kahne, a Houston ACLU attorney, who won the notable *Brooks v. Northglen* HOA case, has written on a HOA Bill of Rights for homeowners. Such a document has been absent from all CC&Rs going back to the *Homes Association Handbook*, TB #50, for the mass merchandising of planned communities, published in 1964 by ULI with the help of federal agencies.

David Kahne's 69 page report, *A BILL of RIGHTS for HOMEOWNERS in ASSOCIATIONS: Basic Principles of*

Consumer Protection and Sample Model Statute can be found here.

The AARP Public Policy Institute, formed in 1985, is part of the Policy and Strategy Group at AARP. One of the missions of the Institute is to foster research and analysis on public policy issues of importance to mid-life and older Americans. This publication represents part of that effort. The views expressed herein are for information, debate, and discussion, and do not necessarily represent official policies of AARP.

III. On the Judiciary

a. Glassel HOA Murders 21 later (2021)

The State of Arizona not only brought the people the Orme School District and the Miranda decisions, but the State also brought the little known Glassel HOA board murders. This April will be the 21st anniversary of sentencing Glassel to death for the shooting murders of two directors, Nila R. Lynn, 69, and Esther LaPlante, 57, at a Ventana Lakes HOA board meeting in April 2000.

I followed this case from the very beginning during my first year as an HOA reform advocate. I had met and talked with Richard Glassel, his wife Susan, his Public Defender, Dr. Jack Potts the psychiatrist who evaluated Glassel as not competent to stand trial, and several reporters; I also attended and observed the 5 day murder trial in 2003.

A few years later about 2010, I don't recall exactly when, I was approached by the *Office of the State Capital Post-*

Conviction seeking my involvement with the Glassel trial. The Office reviews death penalty cases on behalf of the condemned. They asked if I would talk with Glassel, seemingly they were having a problem, and I responded by saying it would not help because I had tried to talk to him on the only day he appeared in court, but he was non-communicative, "living in his own world." Its pending petition for case review was denied as a result of Glassel's death in 2013.

For more detailed coverage, you can follow this *20/20, Dateline, 48 Hours* style murder case at Glassel HOA Murders Redux.

b. Private: Will AZ Supreme Court address broad HOA issues of constitutionality? (2021)

As we approach an October 5th decision to decide to hear the *Tarter v. Bendt* defamation case[i] that raises free speech and limited- purpose public figure issues, I am hoping that the Court will address the real-world widespread misinformation regarding conditions and the legal status of homeowner associations statutes. This investigation by the Court is essential for a just and fair decision in the defamation lawsuit by an HOA president and attorney. Questions of failing to act in good faith and an abuse of the law by the plaintiff attorney with respect to filing a strategic lawsuit against public participation (SLAPP) was raised in my amicus brief.

This is not an ordinary defamation lawsuit but one involving the actions and conduct by the plaintiff in his capacity as the HOA president and in the context of matters of HOA governance. In the recent Nevada Supreme Court opinion in Kosor,[ii] the Court held that "*HOAs as public*

forums and the president as a limited-purpose public figure" and further held that an HOA "*is a quasi-government entity 'paralleling in almost every case the powers, duties, and responsibilities of a municipal government.'*"

The decision by the Arizona Court will have widespread repercussions and consequences not only for Arizona, but for HOAs nationwide affecting statutes in every state. The legitimacy of a democratic country rests on just and fair laws for the people, as Professor Randy Barnett wrote,

A constitution that lacks adequate procedures to ensure the justice of valid laws is illegitimate even if it was consented to by a majority .... A law may be 'valid' because it was produced in accordance with all the procedures required by a particular lawmaking system, [the HOA amendment procedure, for example] but be 'illegitimate' because these procedures were inadequate to provide assurances that a law is just.[iii]

Since the context of the lawsuit relates to the legal status and constitutionality of the HOA model of government, and to the statutes and CC&Rs "constitution" creating private contractual governments, did Bendt receive justice with a $500,000 award for the HOA president's "pain and suffering? As applied to HOA statutes and Acts, will this Court heed US Supreme Court Justice Sotomayor's dissent on the failure to uphold the Constitution?*[iv]*

"Presented with an application to enjoin a flagrantly unconstitutional law engineered to prohibit women from exercising their constitutional rights and evade

judicial scrutiny . . . . Because the Court's failure to act rewards tactics designed to avoid judicial review . . .

"To circumvent it [the Constitution], the [Texas] Legislature took the extraordinary step of enlisting private citizens to do what the State could not . . . . It cannot be the case that a State can evade federal judicial scrutiny by outsourcing the enforcement of unconstitutional laws to its citizenry . . . ."

This case must be remanded to the trial court for consideration of the impact of HOA bias on the decision against Bendt.

c. CC&Rs and waivers of constitutional rights in HOA-Land (2012)

This June 13th extremely important NJ Supreme Court opinion in Mazdabrook deals with the fundamental constitutional question that the homeowner had waived his rights when he agreed to the CC&Rs covenants, which are broadly stated, vague, or implied. I have repeatedly argued that homeowners do not! This opinion will have national impact as other states will follow suit.

Mazdabrook involved the right of a homeowner to place political signs on his private property. **The NJ Supreme court said there was no waiver of free speech rights.**

"Moreover, Khan did not waive his constitutional right to free speech. To be valid, waivers must be knowing, intelligent, and voluntary, and a waiver of constitutional rights in any context must, at the very least, be clear. Khan was not asked to waive his free speech rights; he was asked — by different rules in three documents — to waive the right to post

signs before getting Board approval, without any idea about what standards would govern the approval process. That cannot constitute a knowing, intelligent, voluntary waiver of constitutional rights. . . . . Instead, the exercise of those rights can be subject to reasonable time, place, and manner restrictions. Finally, covenants that unreasonably restrict speech may be declared unenforceable as a matter of public policy. (P. 5)."

In other words, that waiver must meet specific requirements, including an explicit statement of a waiver rather than an broad interpretation or implied waiver as is the current status of CC&Rs. However, understand that rights can be waived if these requirements are met.

"Waiver is the 'intentional relinquishment or abandonment of a known right or privilege.' Although rights may be waived, courts "indulge every reasonable presumption against waiver of fundamental constitutional rights." To be valid, waivers must be knowing, intelligent, and voluntary

The NJ Supreme Court seemed to have educated itself about the spread of CC&Rs with its boiler-plate wording that imply or are interpreted as a waiver, and takes a slap at comment h under § 3.1, Validity of Covenants (Restatement (Third) Property: Servitudes), that argued for the doctrine of equitable servitudes (covenants) to be held superior to the Constitution.

"The proliferation of residential communities with standard agreements that restrict free speech would violate the fundamental free speech values espoused in our Constitution

— the 'highest source of public policy' in New Jersey. (P.11)."

Validity of CC&Rs to bind
Not addressed and unanswered in this opinion is the fundamental question, by extension of what constitutes a waiver, is the question of the validity of the CC&Rs. Is the doctrine of constructive notice sufficient for the CC&Rs to be held as a binding contract? If the CC&Rs are held as invalid, then the question of the waivers of rights becomes moot.

How can the simple notice to the county clerk bind anybody to anything, and be considered a waiver of any right or an agreement to be bound in general? Especially when it is required that, *"To be valid, waivers must be knowing, intelligent, and voluntary."* There is not even a warning in bold, capitalized, large font stating, at purchase time, that the "Taking this deed alone binds you to the CC&Rs sight unseen, without having to read, sign or agree to it."

Background information. This case made references to the Twin Rivers free speech case of 2007, the controlling NJ Schmidt case (as did Twin Rivers), and was also based on violations of the NJ Constitution. Once again, ACLU and The Rutgers Constitutional Law Clinic, Frank Askin Director, filed an amicus curiae brief. NJ CAI filed an amicus in opposition. Both were allowed to present oral arguments on the question of waivers of constitutional rights under HOA CC&Rs. It is legal, but not binding precedent outside of NJ.

See HOA member Declaration of US and State citizenship.

d. No unreasonable HOA expectations (2023)

A healthy democratic society cannot be said to exist without a representative government making fair and just laws. A practical, real-life approach gave rise to the legal concept of reasonableness in an attempt to classify and designate conduct underlying a fair and just administration of the law. The reasonableness doctrine has finally come to HOA disputes in regard to **reasonable expectations**.

CAI has opposed the doctrine of reasonable expectations as too vague, too iffy, and disrupts the order and structure of the HOA "community." In its amicus brief CAI argued that "*reasonableness should be measured by the collective voice, exercising their contractual right to lawfully amend their covenants.*"

The full commentary is a lengthy legal exposition examining 3 Arizona cases on the application of a homeowners' reasonable expectation at time of purchase. Read it here: Reasonableness public policy. "*reasonableness should be measured by the collective voice, exercising their contractual right to lawfully amend their covenants.*"

e. representing yourself in court against HOAs (2015)

An excellent post in the August 15, 2015 L.A. Times column, Associations, by Donie Vanitzian, and co-written by attorney Zachery Levine, contains important information on HOA litigation. Please read it and see what you are up against, and what is needed to have a chance at winning in court. Thanks Donie for all your good work.

An excerpt:

"Success in litigation is based on legal knowledge, resources and organization. Deadlines arise frequently, necessitating quick and timely responses. You are responsible for monitoring what the other side is doing and filing. You must know all applicable deadlines for your case and how to calendar them."

Good luck.

f. Rutgers Journal articles on HOAs and Twin Rivers case (2008)

The current issue of the Rutgers Journal of Law and Public Policy is all about HOAs. See Hannaman Report (NJ)

Rutgers Journal of Law & Public Policy VOLUME 5 SPRING 2008 ISSUE 4

HOMEOWNER ASSOCIATION PROBLEMS AND SOLUTIONS..6
99 **Edward R. Hannaman**, Esq.

THE TWIN RIVERS CASE: OF HOMEOWNERS ASSOCIATIONS, FREE SPEECH RIGHTS AND PRIVATIZED MINI-GOVERNMENTS..7
29

Paula A. Franzese and Steven Siegel

Homeowner Associations: Problems and Solutions, 5 RUTGERS J.L. & PUB. POL'Y 630 (2008).

Excerpts:

"Now, we've learned from society's experience with various policy issues that impact a significant number of people that the path to dealing adequately with the problems begins with talking openly about the problem, confronting reality, and not ignoring it. (Renee Steinhagen, Moderator, p. 631).

"Those trends [public space converted into private space and the privatization of public government functions] lead inexorably to the conclusion that CICs play an increasingly central role in the daily life of New Jersey residents. New Jersey law, however, has continued to regard CICs as wholly private organizations that are largely exempt from any form of regulation or oversight. The *laissez-fare* approach to CIC regulation is reflected in the statutory law, which affords exceedingly few rights and protections to homeowners association residents, and in the common-law principles applied by New Jersey courts when resolving disputes arising over CIC governance. (THE *TWIN RIVERS*1 CASE: OF HOMEOWNERS ASSOCIATIONS, FREE SPEECH RIGHTS AND PRIVATIZED MINI-GOVERNMENTS, Paula A. Franzese and Steven Siegel, p.729)

"One cannot propose solutions without adequately understanding the problems. If society's intention in setting up associations is to encourage the formation of undemocratic Gulags ruled by unaccountable boards and for the enrichment of those who profit from owner ignorance or impotency- we have succeeded completely. (Ed Hannaman, public input, p. 699).

g. Twin Rivers and NJ HOA free speech rights, redux (2011)

Here we go again! Once again revisiting the question of free speech rights to display signs in a New Jersey HOA. In *Mazdabrook v. Khan* the appellate court revisited *Twin Rivers* and the underlying "test case', *State v. Schmidt*, but with a different outcome in favor of free speech. I find it very interesting how our judicial system analyzes and bisects broad legal principles into 1001 "and, if or buts" micro-segments. How is the average person to know what is legal and what is not? Must he go to an attorney, who may or may not know but will take you to court to find out?

In *Mazdabrook* the homeowner placed campaign signs for his election as major of the town, not a for sale sign, but the HOA had governing documents permitting only for sale signs and no others. The court said No, No, No, that's content-based restriction on commercial advertising and a constitutional violation of free speech rights and a total ban on other signs. In contrast to Twin Rivers, the HOA sign restriction to allow a sign in every window and one outside sign no more than three feet from the house was held not to be an unreasonable burden on the owner's free speech rights. It cited the Restatement of Property "suggestion" that a covenant is not valid if it "not

mentioning the obvious that a covenant is also invalid if it were unconstitutional."

See, as to another question of reasonableness, the NJ Esposito case, In NJ, HOA boards do not have to be reasonable, and go figure how our judicial system works. See also the link to the Paula Franzese and Steven Siegel critique of the Twin Rivers decision in Rutgers Journal articles on HOAs and Twin Rivers case.

OF SPECIAL INTEREST and importance is the dissenting opinion of a judge who addressed such questions as: the waiver of one's rights when simply taking possession of his deed, the implied consent to be governed, and a surprising reference to the waiver of ex post facto rights. Where did he get that from??? I wonder?

I've been told that the appellate decision has been appealed to the very same NJ Supreme Court, but oral arguments have not yet been heard. Also, the Rutgers Constitutional Law Clinic under Frank Askin, the party that represented the homeowners in Twin Rivers, has filed an amicus curiae brief for ACLU, and will be allowed to make an oral argument.

Cases

Mazdabrook v. Khan (N.J. Super. A.D., 2010, unpublished).

CBTR v. Twin Rivers, 929 A.2d 1060 (2007).

State v. Schmidt, 423 A.2d 615 (1980).

From NJ Supreme Court Twin Rivers to Dublirer: HOAs separate but unequal governments (2014)

In a parallel that can be made with Plessy v. Ferguson (163 U.S. 537,1896) and its enlightened reversal in *Brown v. Bd of Education* (347 U.S. 483,1954), the NJ Supreme Court's opinion in *Dublirer v. 2000 Linwood Avenue Owners* (2014) accomplished the same necessary correction of its earlier opinion in *CBTW v. Twin Rivers (929 A.2d 1060, 2007)* with respect to HOA constitutionality.

In Plessy, the "separate but equal" doctrine was developed to uphold segregationist laws. In Brown, it was successfully argued that "separate but equal" did not apply to the education of black children and integrated schools were necessary.

(I have read the court filings and briefs in the following cases thanks to the people at the Rutgers Constitutional Litigation Clinic, Frank Askin, Director).

In Twin Rivers, addressing the one issue of many dealing with the equivalent of separate but equal free speech for HOA members, the Court found that alternate means of member free speech was available – that is, the alternate methods were separate but equal – and upheld the constitutionality of the HOA's restrictions. The HOA was not open to the public and was entirely a private entity and not a municipality (factual statement).

The trial court favored the HOA, while the appellate court favored the members. "*In a published opinion, the Appellate Division reversed the trial court, holding that the Association was subject to state constitutional standards with respect to its internal rules and regulations.*"

At the NJ Supreme Court,

Plaintiffs [homeowners] asserted that the community room policy denied them equal protection of the laws and unreasonably and unconstitutionally violated their right to access the community room on a fair and equitable basis. They sought temporary and permanent injunctions "to allow [p]laintiffs to utilize the community room in the same manner as other similarly situated entities.

They urge that political speech is entitled to heightened protection and that they should have the right to post political signs beyond the Association's restricted sign policy. Plaintiffs further contend that the excessive fees charged for the use of the community room are not reasonably related to the actual costs incurred by the Association. Finally, plaintiffs claim that the State Constitution requires that the Association publish plaintiffs' views on an equal basis with which the Association's views are published in its newspaper.

The NJ Supreme Court held,

> "We conclude that the limited nature of the public's invitation to use the property does not favor a finding that the Association's rules and regulations violated plaintiffs' constitutional rights.
>
> "We find that the minor restrictions on plaintiffs' expressional activities are not unreasonable or oppressive, and the Association is not acting as a municipality."

In Dublirer,

The [condo] Board, citing a 'House Rule' that barred soliciting and distributing any written materials, denied the request. On prior occasions, though, the Board had distributed written 'updates' under apartment doors throughout the building, which criticized the Board's opponents. The resident filed a lawsuit and claimed that the House Rule was unconstitutional.

> "The panel [appellate decision] noted that Dublirer's expressional activity was 'political-like speech' because it related to the management and governance of the common-interest community. The panel found that the restriction left Dublirer without reasonable alternative means to convey his message.
>
> "Thus, even though Dublirer did not run for public office, his message was akin to and should be treated as political speech, which is entitled to the highest level of protection in our society. . . . If anything, speech about matters of public interest, and about the qualifications of people who hold positions of trust, lies at the heart of our societal values. . . . We therefore find that the Board's House Rule violates the free speech guarantee in New Jersey's Constitution."

So we see how the NJ Supreme Court recognized the de facto political government nature of HOAs, representing a shift in attitude from 'HOAs are just businesses' agreed to by its members to the need for constitutional protections. The Court essentially declared that the HOA's restrictions in regard to campaigning were not separate but equal methods as used by the board itself. Further, it appears that this Court believes that HOAs are akin to public governments and the election of board members is tantamount to a local public election and must be constitutionally protected.

To ensure that local community government works for the member-owners, shouldn't due process protections and the equal protection of the laws under the 14th Amendment require judicial support and enforcement against HOA violations? And that these rights deserve supremacy over privately drafted contracts that have as their objective the dismissal of constitutional protections? I think so! So should state legislators!

i. Court appointed Receiver files punitive damages against HOA attorney (2011)

In 2008 the DC HOA in Casa Grande, AZ ran into huge debts. It had relied on the advice of its attorney, CAI member Charles Maxwell. In 2009 a homeowner filed for and was granted receivership by the Pinal County court. The court found that an unauthorized removal of some $665,000 from the HOA's bank and ordered Receivership to protect the assets of the HOA. Now, the HOA is being run under the court ordered Receiver.

Last month, the Receiver filed charges of breach of fiduciary duty, breach of ethical duties, disgorgement, professional negligence, aiding and abetting, and breach of contract against the Maxwell & Morgan law firm as well as against Maxwell and his wife, personally.

"Aiding and abetting" is like colluding. "Disgorgement" is asking that the wrong-doers give up their illegally gained profits.

Except for the breach of contract, the above charges are torts — wrongful actions — permitting a claim for punitive damages, which the Receiver is seeking.

Filing tort claims and seeking punitive damages against the HOA and the individual directors is the only effective means today that homeowners have against abusive boards.

Gee, maybe the legislature will see the wisdom of providing its own penalties for wrong doing by abusive HOA boards. Maybe CAI will think this is the smart way to go.

File! File! File tort actions and seek punitive damages before it's too late!

j. IL Supreme Court holds HOAs "are a creature of statute," and not contractual (2014)

Last month the IL Supreme Court opinion in Spanish Court[1] reversed the right of an owner to withhold assessments in view of the HOA's failure to fix and maintain.[2] In its argument, frequently making use of pro-HOA activist and CAI CCAL attorney in Florida, Gary Poliakoff, the Court stated,

> "Although contract principles have sometimes been applied to the relationship between a condominium association and its unit owners based on the condominium's declaration, bylaws, and rules and regulations . . . the relationship is largely a creature of statute, defined by the provisions of the Condominium Act. . . . Although these duties may also be reflected in the condominium declaration and bylaws, as they are in this case, they are imposed by statute and exist independent of the association's governing documents. Accordingly, a unit owner's obligation to pay assessments is not akin to a tenant's purely contractual obligation to pay rent, which

may be excused or nullified because the other party failed to perform. ¶ 21."

So much for the sanctity of the CC&Rs contract! The Court, guided not only by Poliakoff, but by a CAI amicus curiae brief,[3] rolls with the punches and chooses when and when not to uphold the contractual nature of the governing documents.

The Court avoided dealing with the equitable aspects of withholding assessments just like withholding rent, rejecting the favorable appellate decision that held,

> "[T]he obligation to pay assessments, and the obligation to repair and maintain the common elements, as mutually exchanged promises, and concluded that under principles of contract law, a material breach of the repair obligation could warrant nonpayment of assessments. ¶ 7."

Adding fuel to the fire, the Illinois Supreme Court followed the CAI propaganda that the HOA's survival depends on assessments being paid immediately and without question.

> "This section [of the IL condo act] was adopted to provide a constitutionally permissible, quick method for collection of assessment arrearages. . . . The necessity of a "quick method" for collection of past due assessments, unencumbered by extraneous matters, is manifest when we consider the manner in which condominium associations operate . . . . the condominium form of property ownership only works if each unit owner faithfully pays his or her share of the common expenses. When a unit owner defaults in the payment of his or her assessments, the resulting forcible entry and

> detainer action is thus brought "for the benefit of all the other unit owners." ¶¶ 29 - 30.
>
> "Permitting a unit owner's duty to pay assessments to be nullified would thus threaten the financial stability of condominium associations throughout this state. . . . For the same reason that taxpayers may not lawfully decline to pay lawfully assessed taxes because of some grievance or claim against the taxing governmental unit, a condominium unit owner may not decline to pay lawful assessments. Trustees of the Prince Condominium Trust v. Prosser, 592 N.E.2d 1301." ¶ 32.

Here we have the alleged dicta [non-supported court opinions], and becoming part of the Illinois public policy, that the survival of the HOA/condo is first and foremost. The HOA rises to the same level as a public entity, with the questionable governing documents now having contractual validity and court support to deny homeowner rights, freedoms, privileges and immunities.

Welcome to the New America of HOA-Land.

References

[1] http://www.state.il.us/court/Opinions/SupremeCourt/2014/115342.pdf.
[2] See appellate decision Court decisions: HOA Enlightenment Movement vs. the Dark Ages.
[3] "*Spanish Court Condominium Association II vs. Carlson* (Illinois)," CAI Amicus Curiae Activity 2013.

Advocate files AZ supreme court amicus brief (2023)

We must make the injustice visible.
We must provoke until they respond and change the laws.
(Mahatma Gandhi)

An AZ supreme court amicus brief was filed by Jonathan Dessaules on behalf of the *Arizona Homeowners Coalition in CAO v. Dorsey (CA-CV 21-0275)* (Waiting for the Court's decision). Dessaules argues that the statute in question, ARS 33-1228, conflicts with the Arizona Constitution, Article 2, Section 17, and "*a statute cannot circumvent or modify constitutional requirements*".

The intricate legality and constitutionality of private entities—the HOA — taking of another party's property rights – a homeowners — is discussed in detail. I frequently quote the brief to ensure accuracy in my review.

ARS 33-1228 "*allows condominium associations to force the sale of a nonconsenting owner's property for someone else's private use*" and is the justification for investors to shut down the HOA. However, "*When a state statute conflicts with Arizona's Constitution, the constitution must prevail.*"

Furthermore, it is argued that "*The legislature may not enact a statute which is in conflict with a provision of the Arizona Constitution." Consequently, the Legislature lacked the authority to enact 33-1228.*"

(Stay with it!) The brief goes on to say that ARS 12-1131 provides that "*eminent domain may be exercised only if the use of eminent domain is authorized by this state, whether by statute or otherwise, and for a public use as defined in this article.*" Public use does not allow for "forcing the sale of a holdout owner's property to be used by the investor who owners a majority of the other units within the condominium."

The HOA, Dorsey, counterclaimed that it wasn't a sovereign and § 1231 doesn't apply to private organizations, ignoring § 12-1111 that permits individuals the right of eminent domain takings. Consequently, again, it is argued that 12-1228 is invalid.

An additional powerful argument is raised that the Declaration is an adhesion contract. "A declaration is generally a '*standardized form offered to consumers on essentially a take it or leave it basis.*'" And to my long awaited legality, the brief states that *"Without the contract even being presented to the purchaser for their signature,"* the contract is imposed on the buyer.

Again, we see the doctrine of "reasonable expectations" as applied to adhesion contracts. "Contracts of adhesion will not be enforced unless they are conscionable and within the reasonable expectations of the parties." Dessaules maintains that including unconstitutional statutes in the Condo Act is "substantively unconscionable." Furthermore, as I have argued many times, "*a waiver of a constitutional right is not within reasonable expectations of the parties.*"

This is a solid amicus brief by an advocate fighting for HOA reforms to protect members' rights and privileges. It does not pretend to accept unjust laws.

* * * *

I would like to thank Dennis Legere, Arizona Homeowners Coalition, for hiring attorney Jonathan Dessaules to file this important, to the point, excellent amicus brief.

AZ amicus brief seeking answers to constitutional)A questions denied (2014)

A constitutionality challenge[1] was made to Arizona's SB 1482 "HOA Omnibus Bill" (ominous bill), the 2014 version of SB 1454 from last year.[2] Although the law has become effective this past July 24th, the case is still active. Yours truly filed an amicus curiae brief in superior court on behalf of the Pro Se plaintive, Dave Russell, to which the Arizona Attorney General, lawyer for the State of Arizona, found objectionable. The judge denied my motion to file the brief.

The AG objected under a too one-sided against Arizona argument (complete objection).

> "Defendant, State of Arizona, opposes George K. Starapoli's Motion for Leave to File Amicus
>
> "Brief in this matter for the following reasons:
>
> "1. There is no authority to file an Amicus Brief in this matter in the superior court.
>
> "2. It would be prejudicial to the State to allow the brief to be filed at this time. The State has responded to the Plaintiffs Motion for Expedited Preliminary Injunction, and that Motion could be considered based on the documents already filed by the parties. To allow the brief to be filed would prolong the process, require additional response, and potentially confuse the issues."

I did not refer to the Injunction, but the complaint itself, so what gives?? What does "*potentially confuse the issues"* mean? Too much for the AG or judge to handle???

<u>On the 28th, the judge ruled (complete minute entry),</u>

> "On July 11, 2014, George Staropoli filed a 'Motion for Leave to File an Amicus Curiae Brief in Support of the Plaintiff'. The Court has reviewed this motion and considered the circumstances. Under the circumstances,
>
> IT IS ORDERED denying the above-identified motion."

What does "under the circumstances mean????? Was it too confusing for the court to handle????

I was informed that a leading public interest nonprofit that has argued before the Arizona Supreme Court has had its amicus briefs to the Superior Court also denied. I expected as much, but I had hoped for a dissertation as to why the denial beyond "under the circumstances."

The issues that I raised in my amicus brief were:

> "Is a bill allowing HOA managers to represent HOAs while prohibiting the homeowner to engage an unlicensed and untrained third-party to speak for them in small claims court an unconstitutional special law in violation of the equal protection of the law under the US and Arizona Constitutions? (SB 1482, Section 7).
>
> "Do the renter documentation requirements and restrictions constitute an unconstitutional interference with private agreements as it creates more harm to the homeowners than the benefits of an

unstated government interest? (SB1482, Sections 11 and 15)."

The court must still decide on the injunction to not enforce the bill (or the part dealing with HOA managers in small claims court), which it cannot do because Rule 31 of the Arizona Supreme Court forbids non-lawyers from representing anyone in court, including small claims court. And the Constitution says the SC controls its procedures and not the legislature! So, folks, what's the fuss all about?

What this incident has demonstrated is the use of the law by the AG and an eagerly cooperative court. Was my brief so harmful to the State of Arizona's case that the truth must be hidden? Or was my brief valid because the overwhelming facts and background presented made a strong case for *the tyranny of the legislature* that resulted in an unconstitutional law, a law which was motivated by domineering HOA stakeholders, the special interests?

What my little exercise has demonstrated is the silence on the part of our government. Why? Because like an HOA they don't have too! A law is constitutional because the 'sovereign,' the legislature, has spoken and can do no wrong. Like an HOA, the state well knows it cannot make a valid and compelling justification for the bill in question, SB 1482. Any such attempt would demonstrate to all that **the State of Arizona was** *defending the indefensible.* So, mum's the word.

How does a citizen successfully argue his case when the State's defense is, "Because I can!"

References

[1] See the complaint, *Russell v. State of Arizona*, CV2014-093-052 (Maricopa County Superior Court).

[2] See in general: A lesson in HOA reforms and power politics in AZ; AZ legislature fails to remove invalid statutes from its ARS web page.

m. AZ Supreme Court accepts advocate's amicus challenge to HOA statute (2011)

The Arizona Supreme Court has accepted my amicus curiae brief in support of constitutionality of the DFBLS/OAH due process statutes (*Gelb v. DFBLS*, CV 10-0371-PR). The Court has yet to decide if it will hear the Petition from the homeowner. Neither party objected to my brief, not even the CAI HOA law firm that received harsh treatment. I had presented background facts and arguments in an effort to assist the Court in understanding the disgraceful state of affairs with HOAs.

Responses to my brief, if any, are due within 20 days. For over 10 years I've been waiting for the CAI HOA attorneys to debate the substantive, constitutional issues with me for all to see. I await their response.

The excerpt below makes a strong accusation against the Arizona Legislature, which can be applied to all state legislatures. Given this posture, I would like to thank those all too few individual legislators who had come forth over the years, in several states, to do battle for homeowner justice, but who were not sufficient to overcome the opposition in their legislatures. Your efforts are very much appreciated.

From the first paragraph of my Conclusion:

> "It is quite evident that an Arizona homeowner living within an HOA governed subdivision cannot look to the Attorney General, the Legislature, DFBLS, or ADRE (real estate dept.) for due process protections

> and the equal application of the laws. Even the lower courts are suspect. With all due respect, it remains to this Court to stand behind the promises and covenants between our system of government and the people as set forth in the U.S. and state Constitutions."

See Advocate submits amicus brief in AZ supreme court appeal of HOA due process, and for a copy of the amicus brief, Amicus.

Congress of the United States

The Preamble to The Bill of Rights

THE Conventions of a number of the States, having at the time of their adopting the Constitution, expressed a desire, in order to prevent misconstruction or abuse of its powers, that further declaratory and restrictive clauses should be added:

IV. On Civics

a. HOAs are another form of local government (2021)

Listening to the events concerning the shooting in Brooklyn Center, MN I was surprised to learn that its form of government is based on the council-manager system. We are more familiar with the mayor – council or mayor – manager forms of local government where the mayor is elected and plays a major role in governing the city.[1]

However, in the council-manager form the mayor is a figure head with the powers to rule the city are divided between the elected city council and a city manager appointed by the council. Sound familiar? Many HOA Bylaws follow the council-manager form of local government, except that the Bylaws do provide for corporation laws governing the duties of officers. This is true of the many large HOAs and the retirement/resort subdivisions.

The division of labor and authority follows the public form in that the council holds ultimate responsibility for the conduct of the government but is restricted to policy issues, while the appointed manager actually runs the HOA. A good example can be found in an Arizona active-adult HOA of some 17,000 people.

> **"The affairs of the Association shall be managed by a Board of Directors which shall serve as the corporate policy-making body of the Association. . . . The Board is not**

responsible for nor authorized to perform day-to-day operations of the Association. The day-to-day operations of the Association shall be carried out by CAM or agents retained by the Association under the supervision of the Board.

"Subject to the Board's responsibilities concerning operational policies, it shall be the policy of the Association . . . that the Board refrain from unreasonably interfering with the performance of delegated functions by CAM."

The major difference between local public government Brooklyn Center, MN and the Arizona HOA lies in the private contractual nature of the HOA that absolves it from application of the US Constitution as well as the state constitution. HOA members are, as compared to non-HOA members, therefore second-class citizens lacking constitutional protections within their own state.[2]

The $64,000 question is: So why is there so much opposition to requiring the HOA to be subject to the Constitution like all other forms of local government? **BEFORE you respond**, think very carefully with respect to the implication and consequences of your response.

References

[1] See in general, Roger L. Kemp, "Forms of Governance," *Managing America's Cities: A Handbook for Local Government Productivity*, McFarland & Co., (2007). They are: Strong Mayor, Council-Manager, Town Meeting (direct or representative democracy), and Commission. See

also, Home rule doctrine vs. HOA governments; CC&Rs are a devise for de facto HOA governments to escape constitutional government.
[2] See George K. Staropoli, **HOA-Land Nation Within America** *(2019).*

b. CC&Rs are a devise for de facto HOA governments to escape constitutional government (2015)

This commentary takes a long look at the validity of HOA covenants and the need for judicial enforcement in order to invoke state action with respect to fundamental rights and freedoms. It informs the reader that such enforcement depends upon the member's voluntary agreement to be bound by the declaration, and raises issues of the lack of genuine agreement. The agreement requirement is not analyzed under contract law, but under HOA law that has been designed to protect the HOA and position the declaration as the supreme law of the HOA community.

Long ago in 1994 Professor McKenzie wrote, *"HOAs currently engage in many activities that would be prohibited if they were viewed by the courts as the equivalent of local governments.*[i]

Two years after *Marsh v. Alabama*[ii] — the 1946 Supreme Court opinion setting the misguided "public functions" test for a municipality — the Court specifically dealt with the question of the constitutionality of restrictive covenants. The issue in *Shelly v. Kraemer*[iii] was *"that judicial enforcement of the restrictive agreements in these cases has violated rights guaranteed to petitioners by the Fourteenth Amendment."*

With respect to restrictive covenant enforcement the Shelly court said: *"That the action of state courts and of judicial officers in their official capacities is to be regarded as action of the State ['state action'] within the meaning of the Fourteenth Amendment, is a proposition which has long been established by decisions of this Court. . . . The federal guaranty of due process extends to state action through its judicial as well as through its legislative, executive, or administrative branch of government."* The Court held *"that in granting judicial enforcement of the restrictive agreements in these cases,* ***the States have denied petitioners the equal protection of the laws*** *and that, therefore, the action of the state courts cannot stand"* (my emphasis).

Unfortunately, the Court chose a narrow view of this issue limiting it to that involving racial discrimination. A more expansive application of the 14th Amendment can easily be applied to any covenant that violates a member's rights, freedoms or privileges and immunities as a citizen, but that has not been the case.

The 1976 Florida case, *Brock v. Watergate Mobile Home*,[iv] directly addressed the question of an HOA declaration and its actions under the Declaration. It used the *Marsh* "public functions" test and the additional "close nexus" test (HOA action is closely resembles government action). No state action was found. The HOA was not like a company town and the state's involvement, as occurred in the limited context of the case, was not a close nexus.

Please understand that CC&RS and covenants are not automatically invalid or unconstitutional. It requires a court to declare them so, at the expense of a homeowner lawsuit.

Also, it is important to note that the court question was not about the validity of a restrictive covenant itself, but the court enforcement of that covenant. (This requires a lawsuit in which the court upholds the covenant and a subsequent lawsuit charging a violation of the 14th Amendment.) The Shelly court's view was that as the 14th Amendment applied *"only to governmental action, as contrasted to action of private individuals, there was no showing that the covenants, which were simply agreements between private property owners, were invalid."* **Furthermore,** *"[The 14th] Amendment erects no shield against merely private conduct, however discriminatory or wrongful"*. In Arizona, today, the appellate court is to decide whether a CAI attorney amendment to Terravita's CC&Rs that directly contradicts state law will be held valid.[v] Behold the power of private contracts!

In view of the above we can ask, what makes a valid agreement? Fortunately, a condition was attached to this view, which is never ever mentioned by pro-HOA supporters including those renowned CAI attorneys: "***So long as the purposes of those agreements are effectuated by voluntary adherence to their terms.***" Sadly the courts have unquestionably accepted the validity of the CC&Rs as a voluntary agreement and this *consent to be bound* has become legal doctrine. For example, in *Midlake v. Cappuccio* the PA appellate court upheld a valid *consent to agree* by the buyer at time of purchase: *"The Cappuccios contractually agreed to* *abide by the provisions in the Declaration at the time of purchase, thereby relinquishing their freedom of speech concerns regarding placing signs on this property."*[vi] There have been numerous other cases where the court has upheld a valid *consent to agree* per se and a waiver/surrender of constitutional rights under said holding.

But, is there a genuine *consent to agree*? I have written several commentaries about the lack of a genuine consent to agree as a result of misrepresentation, fraud, half-truths and hidden factors not fully disclosed to homebuyers.[vii] Certainly not according to contract law 101 with its requirements for full disclosure, a *meeting of the minds*, and absence of fraud.

Unfortunately, once again, HOA declarations and covenants are seen as a law unto themselves that is based on a cutting and pasting of various laws, including constitutionality law, to provide for the protection and survival of HOAs. We have pro-HOA statutes in every state and a *Restatement of Servitudes**[viii]*** (covenants) that was written to promote and protect HOAs. "*Therefore this Restatement is enabling toward private government, **so long as there is full disclosure**"*[ix] (my emphasis).

The *Restatement* advises judges — and is regarded as precedent — that its collection of laws known as HOA law dominates all others. Section 6.13, comment a, states: *"The question whether a servitude unreasonably burdens a fundamental constitutional right is determined as a matter of property law, and not constitutional law". Section* 3.1, comment h, states: *"in the event of a conflict between servitudes law and the law applicable to the association form, servitudes law should control."*

And we have CAI, the national HOA lobbying organization, repeatedly making it clear that the HOA is a city-state, an independent principality, and the decisions of the HOA are the supreme law of the community.[x] It is easily concluded why CAI has vehemently denied and opposed any reference or declaration that HOAs are de facto governments — mini or quasi-governments — and argue that HOAs remain free from constitutional restrictions on government entities.

HOAs have been institutionalized under this state of affairs, this public policy, and unquestionably accepted as *this is the way it is.* Nothing will improve the conditions to which HOA residents are subject unless HOA public policy changes. Public policy today rejects constitutional government for HOAs and allows HOAs to operate outside the law of the land.

The policy makers fail to understand that the terms and conditions of the HOA CC&Rs cross over the line between purely property restrictions to establishing unregulated and authoritarian private governments.

References

[i] Evan McKenzie, *Privatopia: Homeowners Associations and the Rise of Residential Private Governments,* Yale Univ. Press, 1994.
[ii] *Marsh v. Alabama,* 326 U.S. 501 (1946). The holding was that a company town was no different from a municipal town.
[iii] *Shelly v. Kraemer,* 334 U.S. 1 (1948).
[iv] *Brock v. Watergate Mobile Home,* 502 So. 2d 1380 (Fla. 4th Dist. App. 1987). This case was a

civil rights violations case based on 42 US 1983 as a result of various acts by the HOA.

[v] *Brown v. Terravita*, 1 CA-CV 14-455. See Will Arizona allow HOA covenants to dominate state laws? and Does the Constitution support the will of the HOA no matter what?

[vi] *Midlake v. Cappuccio*, 673 A.2d 340 (Pa.Super. 1996) (PA appellate court). .

[vii] See "Consent to be governed, No. 4," **HOA Common Sense: rejecting private government;** Proposed "consent to be governed" statute, the "Truth in HOAs" bill; and court examines consent and surrender of rights in HOA CC&Rs.

[viii] *Restatement Third, Property: Servitudes* (American Law Institute 2000).

[ix] *Id.*, From the Forward: *"Professor Susan French [Reporter (chief editor/contributor) for this Restatement] begins with the assumption . . . that we are willing to pay for private government because we believe it is more efficient than [public] government . . . . Therefore this Restatement is enabling toward private government, so long as there is full disclosure . . . ."*

[x] See CAI: the HOA form of government is independent of the US Constitution; Misrepresentation: CAI comes with unclean hands and Will the real CAI standup: its contradictory beliefs, pronouncements and goals.

c. Combined Advocate Surveys vs. CAI surveys (2016)

Let the truth be known!

Two homeowner rights advocates, Sara Benson (Chicago) and Jill Schweitzer (Phoenix), were responsible for 2 online polls on homeowner satisfaction with HOAs.[i] In stark contrast, not surprisingly, the Combined Advocate Surveys, as I refer to them, revealed opinions and views refuting the results of the CAI "happiness" surveys.[ii] It appears that the CAI studies were happiness studies of happy HOA members.

Under the trade name, *George Analytics*,[iii] a proprietary investigation and analysis of the 3 surveys was conducted and standard statistical T Tests for validity were applied. Some observations: both the CAI and Combined surveys were internet polls (CAI included telephone calling) consisted of a reported 800 responses. CAI's questions were more generalized and less detailed than the enquiring questions in the Combined surveys, which, naturally, provided more insights into HOA issues and controversies.

Because of the variations in the questions asked and response alternatives provided, some 'reworking' was in order. Consequently, a 'favorable to HOA' vs. 'unfavorable to HOA' category was adopted and the responses placed accordingly. For example, a YES response could be pro-HOA or not depending on the wording of the question. Three sets of responses are used as examples: yes/no, like/favor/prefer, and positive/negative with respect to favorable or unfavorable. To avoid the yes/no example above, I had to rephrase some questions so that 'yes,' for example, was always a favorable, pro-HOA response.

In statistical terms, the *George Analytics* table below shows that the CAI and Combined responses (average percentages) come from 2 distinct samples, segments, of the HOA population at a 99.5% significance level.

	favorable	**unfavorable**
combined advocate response	8%	79%
CAI response	59%	15%

Now, in laymen's terms, what does this mean and how can this wide gap in views be reconciled? First, the lauded CAI surveys do not represent the complete population of HOA members as claimed by CAI[iv], and these surveys cannot be promoted as representing reality within HOA-Land. They are tainted! So too, for that matter, are the Combined surveys. However, they are valid within themselves and also serve the important purpose of refuting the results of all those CAI surveys that CAI now claims to have been validated. As CAI proclaimed,

> *The findings objectively refute the unfounded and unsubstantiated myth that the community association model of governance is failing to serve the best interests of Americans who choose to live in common-interest communities.[v]*

Not so!

The findings from the six surveys are strikingly consistent and rarely vary a standard margin error for national, demographically representative surveys.[v]

This is a meaningless statement. What does 'rarely vary a standard margin of error' (the commonly seen "+/-n" footnotes to political polls) mean? It refers to the internal consistency of the polled samples and has only meaning as being representative only if there are statistics relating to a survey sample representing all HOA members. The Combined Advocate Surveys demonstrate that the CAI surveys are not representative of all HOA members.

Call to Action!
To truly validate its surveys CAI must reject the findings of the Combined Advocate Surveys, not by hyperbole or by rhetoric, but by opening up to a bona fide study of HOA-Land by independent researchers. And state governments must cry out for this independent study to end its lack of awareness of conditions and stress within HOA-Land.

The Truth Is Out There!

References

[i] Combined Advocate Surveys — Sara Benson: Chppi's 2015 National HOA Survey; Jill Schweitzer's HOA Industry Survey.
[ii] CAI 2016 National Homeowner Survey,
[iii] HOA Surveys Comparison.
[iv] *Supra ii.*
[v] *Supra ii.*

d. KC Star: problem with HOA? Don't go to CAI (2016)

KC Star HOA articles by Judy Thomas, Aug. 3, 2016 Please read these articles that do not hide the facts about HOA-Land.

The KC Star HOA articles, Aug. 3, 2016
Do you have a homeowners association story to share? Let us know, Kansas City Star Have you had

positive or negative experiences to share about your homeowners association?
Kansas City Star reporters would like to hear them Group shifts its mission — and homeowners get left behind,
Kansas City Star If you're looking for help because your homeowners association is pushing you around, there's one place you may not want to go: The Community ...
HOAs from hell: Homes associations that once protected residents now torment them,
Kansas City Star "Door after door, complaints about the homeowners association were laid upon ... at War:
The Creepy Case Against Your Homeowners Association.". Garage doors can't be cordovan — and more odd HOA stories,
Kansas City Star Last year, when it was time to paint again, she decided to stick with the cordovan trim, and her son, Ken, got the homeowners association's approval. You can run an HOA well, even after vowing to never live in one again,
Kansas City Star Ed McHardie gets it when he hears horror stories about life in a homeowners association. He has a story of his own. In fact, he once vowed to never ... Critics say many avenues can lead to reforming the HOA mess,
Kansas City Star The CAI says a registry can become a financial burden on a homeowners association. Charging "per door" fees for registration is not fair, it says, and

e. ASU Law ignores content-neutral free speech for HOAs (2020)

Much to my disappointment, the ASU Law library has not responded to my 3 emails[i] requesting an HOA advocate resource listing on its Homeowner

Associations resource webpage. Under Books CAI attorney member Scott Carpenter is listed (reference is to an AZ Bar Assn booklet on HOA law, and under Websites AACM (community manager association) is listed.

Both of these listings carry the lobbying view found in the *CAI School of HOA Governance.[ii]* Neither address constitutional issues nor do they contain the views of constitutional lawyers. There is a constitutional issue at play as I informed the librarian and the Law School Dean — the illegal bias toward one party's content while denying another party's material content. The law requires content-neutral free speech which I believe is being violated by ASU. So, as I proposed, remove these listings, or add my books and web pages or those of other homeowner rights advocates.

How can law students from the prestigious *Sandra Day O'Connor School of Law* obtain access to material information concerning the long ignored HOA legal scheme that, apparently, ASU does not agree with? Change cannot occur in the blind! There cannot be change without change!

PS: I am waiting for a response from The Uniform Law Commission (ULC) that is drafting updates to UCIOA. Its Scope Committee is reviewing my request for ULC study of my proposal for an HOA Member Bill of Rights; it will meet again in January.

NOTES

[i] *Copy of email letter*

gKS256@nyu.edu

To: Beth DIFelice (beth.difelice@asu.edu)
CC:
'douglas.sylvester@asu.edu'; Diana.Bowman@asu.edu
November 11, 2020

Email letter

Beth DiFelice
Director ASU Law Library
Sandra Day O'Connor College of Law
Arizona State University

Dear Director, DiFelice,

I am sorry to say that I am disappointed in not receiving a courtesy acknowledgement of my two emails regarding my request for "equal time" as a homeowner association resource on the library's web page — books and websites. It seems that the First Amendment issue at play here with respect to the regulation of content-based free speech has not been recognized. ASU provides lobbying special interests, CAI and AACM, along with others of the same views and positions and, by your silence, ASU denies my views with which, apparently, you and ASU do not agree.

As I emailed on October 21st and November 3rd, by not providing ASU law students with access to views opposed to those of your resource listings, ASU is sending off its law students, to be blunt, half-cocked. How can students fairly represent homeowners living in HOAs if all they have only been exposed to the prevailing biased views of the special interests? As argued by the links and references provided in my request, your displayed references support the view that HOAs are independent of the Constitutional protections guranteed for all citizens; my references contain legitmate and valid primary and secondary legal authorites.

I hope ASU Law will consider my request and do the right thing: either remove the content-based references or add my books and web pages, among those of others, on the constitutionality of the HOA legal scheme.

Respectfully,

George K. Staropoli
Founder

[ii] The foundation and principles of the *School* can be traced back to CAI's Public Policies, The *CAI Manifesto* (its 2016 "white paper"), its numerous seminars and conferences, its Factbooks and surveys, its amicus briefs to the courts, and its advisories, letters, emails, newsletters, blogs etc. I have designated

these foundations and principles collectively as the *CAI School of HOA Governance.*

f. HOA advocate to advise committee on CIOA revision (2020)

I was invited to participate in the drafting of revisions to the Uniform Law Commission's (ULC) *Uniform Common Interest Ownership Act* (UCIOA) and Uniform Condominium Act (UCA). As an invited Observer with full participation rights I bring "in the trenches" in-depth experience and extensive research to *restore the lost Constitution* to HOA-Land.

With the advocates' failure to nationally unite and collaborate to attain substantive HOA reforms, going forward with ULC's statewide collaborative approach will benefit all interested parties, including HOA members. The drafting committee is comprised of conscientious and dedicated unpaid volunteer attorneys appointed by their state. Uniform Acts (UCC for example) adopted by ULC are presented to state legislators to adopt and to ease the disorder brought about by different rules in different states that affect a person's home in an HOA.

My late 12 hour introduction into the amend and revise procedure allowed me to orient myself to the functioning of the UCIOA committee as well as presenting a few points of view. The proposed UCIOA changes are in the review process and need to be approved by the ULC commissioners at their annual meeting, yet to be determined as a result of the coronavirus restrictions.

When and if future revisions to UCIOA are in order I hope to participate more fully.

g. Uniform Law Commission rejects subjecting HOAs to Constitution (2020)

Today I received a telephone rejection from ULC on my proposal for an HOA Members Bill of Rights. It comes a day after my Commentary on ASU Law silence containing a statement that there has not been a ULC response, some 3 weeks after ULC's Oct. 29 meeting.

> *"I am waiting for a response from The Uniform Law Commission (ULC) that is drafting updates to UCIOA. Its Scope Committee is reviewing my request for ULC study of my proposal for an HOA Member Bill of Rights; it will meet again in January."*

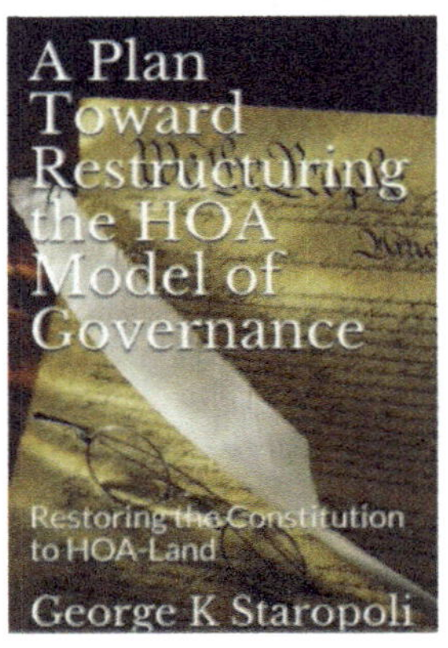

Nothing in writing, nothing formal, just a phone call. The essentials of the call, after a short debate where we could not reach an eye-to-eye understanding of what my point was, is very disappointing.

> *"I appreciate your call and our discussion on my rejected proposal. I think we are too far apart at this time: 'not functionally useful for lawyers,' and 'not workable.'" The Scope Committee and editorial board "had difficulty in seeing HOAs as a government."*

In this call I stressed my proposed statute that would mandate HOAs to be subject to the Constitution like any other local government; the response was, "*they didn't see how that would help.*"

Long ago The Founding Fathers rejected the patchwork approach to modifying the *Articles of Confederation* and replaced it with a complete rewrite — The US Constitution and the Bill of Rights. It's well beyond time that the HOA "constitution," the CC&Rs, be replaced in its entirety as proposed in *A Plan Toward Restructuring the HOA Model of Governance.*

h. Is CAI a coercive monopoly? Definitely YES! (2023)

Consider the FTC's lawsuit that Amazon is a coercive monopoly.

> *"The US government and 17 states are suing Amazon in a landmark monopoly case reflecting years of allegations that the e-commerce giant abused its economic dominance and harmed fair competition. Because of Amazon's dominance in e-commerce, sellers have little option but to accept Amazon's terms, the FTC alleges.*
>
> *"Amazon is 'squarely focused on preventing anyone else from gaining that same critical mass of customers,' FTC Chair Lina Khan told reporters Tuesday.*

> *"In a release, Khan accused Amazon of using 'punitive and coercive tactics' to preserve an illegal monopoly. 'Amazon is now exploiting its monopoly power to enrich itself. . . Today's lawsuit seeks to hold Amazon to account for these monopolistic practices and restore the lost promise of free and fair competition.'"*

These charges of monopoly and coercive tactics can be applied to the Community Associations Institute's (CAI) long pattern of conduct with respect to the domination of the homeowners associations industry. In my 40-page complaint to the DOJ in January 2023 I laid out the case that CAI must have its conduct curtailed in the interest of free competition in Housing and in educational services used to maintain its monopoly.

My recommendations to regulate CAI's activities to allow for the voice of others to be heard, especially from owners of HOA homes who suffer under the monopoly, as included in my complaint, are listed here: The need to regulate CAI monopoly.

> "A. Regulations on CAI's monopolistic activities
> "B. Regulations on HOA activities in support of CAI monopoly"

What is needed now? **Support my anti-trust complaint against CAI!**

i. **"Beyond Privatopia" – understanding the economic theories that brought about the New America of HOA-Land Restructuring the HOA model (2011)**

Once again, a short book, 168 pages, by McKenzie is packed with very important information for those seriously interested in understanding the HOA phenomenon. A must reading for the public interest nonprofits, the legal-academic aristocrats, and all state legislators who have failed over the years to face the realities of the social and political impact of HOAs on our democratic system of government.

In his Preface, McKenzie proclaims that "*this book is written in my own unusual hybrid perspective*", having one foot in the legal-academic club and the other foot amongst the homeowner rights advocates. He names names of leading advocates (p. 121, n. 4): Shu Bartholomew, Jan Bergemann, Pat Haruff, George Starapoli [sic], Fred Pilot and Monica Sadler.

Yet, my impression so far is that the book is addressed to the legal-academic aristocrats to remind them that America was not founded on the state being an neoclassic economic force, a business, concerned with efficiency, productivity, wealth redistribution, or rational choice But, that America was founded on principles of democratic government as set forth in the Preamble to the US Constitution (my interpretation):

> *We the People of the United States, in Order to form a more perfect Union, establish Justice, insure domestic*

> *Tranquility, provide for the common defense, promote the general Welfare, and secure the Blessings of Liberty to ourselves and our Posterity . . . .*

In Chapter 3 McKenzie discusses the libertarian views of Robert H. Nelson and Nozick, among others. He references Nelson with, *"They contend that CIDs* [McKenzie's generic term for HOAs] *are more efficient and more democratic* [my emphasis] *than municipalities and should replace them."* (p. xi). He present's Nozick's 1974 argument (p. 47) for *"minimal states"* that lead to *"private protective associations."* Minimal states and protective associations have become today's call for less public government and the CC&Rs enforcement agency known as the HOA.

Nozick's defense of minimal states, according to McKenzie, is that *"This* [minimal] *state would be legitimate, even though it may infringe on the liberty of individuals* [my emphasis], *because from the bottom up it would have been based on voluntarism and the rights of contract."* Sounds eerie doesn't it? We hear these arguments today in defense of the HOA legal scheme, but as McKenize argued, they are based on myths. *"The notion that individual owners agreed among themselves to perform these services for each other, and subsequent owners took over from them, is entirely fictional."* (p. 60).

Enough for now. More to come . . . .

Beyond Privatopia: Rethinking Residential Private Government, Evan McKenzie (Urban Inst. 2011).

j. HOAs need major restructuring (2020)

> *Whether you like your HOA, or dislike your HOA, is immaterial. It's all about the Constitution and the HOA legal scheme. What matters is whether the HOA legal structure is a danger to the country, because it will happen again. And none of us can have confidence, based on the historical record, that it will not happen again because . . . every day it is allowed to continue at will.*[1]

It is well past the time for a restructuring of the HOA model of local government formulated some 56 years ago by ULI in 1964 — *The Homes Association Handbook*. In 1973 CAI was formed to deal with the persistent problems facing the HOA model, and in 1992 CAI was forced to change its educational tax-exempt status to that of a business trade group in an attempt to deal with the continued problems with HOA.[2] In 2005 it had to drop HOAs as a member due to conflicts with the purpose of a business trade group — HOAs are consumers of CAI services.

These HOA problems and issues are endemic to the legal model of unconstitutional, private governments as a result of the intents and motivations behind the introduction of HOAs: to make $$$ by means of a mass merchandising effort.[3] Constitutional considerations were ignored and avoided by focusing on the legalities of real estate law and equitable servitudes to justify the legal authority over the HOA members. The policy makers have failed to understand that the HOA CC&Rs have crossed over the line between purely property restrictions to establishing unregulated and authoritarian private governments.

There is no denying that the HOA subdivision managed by competent boards and professionals appeals to the desires and wants of home buyers and bring many benefits. It comes as no surprise that the vast majority of persons living in an HOA approve and love their HOA, finding only minor problems with the board of directors or HOA managers. The annual "satisfaction" surveys produced by the pro-HOA trade group, CAI, reflect this positive attitude.

However, the HOA legal structure and scheme is authoritarian in nature: strong central power, limited political freedoms, no accountability, and under the rule of man, not law.

> *But the HOA is truly a totalitarian democracy. A totalitarian democratic state is said to maximize its control over the lives of its citizens by using the dual rationale of general will (i.e., "public good") and majority rule.[4]*

Prof. McKenzie wrote in 1994: *"HOAs currently engage in many activities that would be prohibited if they were viewed by the courts as the equivalent of local governments."[5]* The authoritarian nature of HOA-Land is masked by a thorough indoctrination that presents a false picture of the real estate subdivision as democratic, inappropriately named a community, simply because the members are allowed to vote, as meaningless as it is.

The HOA danger to the Constitution has been presented in several Commentaries herein, and in the *white paper* found in the book, *The HOA-Land Nation Within America.***[6]**

> *There is no denying that the HOA subdivision managed by competent boards and professionals appeals to the desires and wants of home buyers and bring many benefits. However, as this whitepaper addresses, the means to this end are highly suspect and harmful to our democratic system of government.*

HOA management consulting

StarMan Group, HOA Management Consulting, offers a program to resolve many of the substantive defects with HOAs by means of the complete restructuring of the model: a program of organizational development. It also requires the removal of the adverse influences by the *CAI School of HOA Governance* as I collectively refer to CAI's policies, best practices, guides, communications, seminars and certifications, and in its Manifesto.[7]

References

[1] Rep. Schiff's (Rep. Adam Schiff is the leading Democratic impeachment prosecutor), opening argument Friday, Jan. 24, 2020, appealing to the Senators to uphold the Constitution. *"Whether you like the president, or dislike the president, is immaterial. It's all about the Constitution and his misconduct. What matters is whether he is a danger to the country, because he will do it again. And none of us can have confidence, based on his record, that he will not do it again because he is telling us every day that he will."*

[2] See in general: Evan McKenzie, *Privatopia: Homeowners Associations and the Rise of Residential Private Governments,* Yale Univ. Press, 1994; Donald R. Stabile, *Community Associations: The Emergence and Acceptance of a Quiet Innovation in Housing (funded by CAI and ULI).*
[3] See in general, "*Analysis of The Homes Association Handbook,*" *George K. Staropoli (2006).*
[4] George K. Staropoli, *The HOA-Land Nation Within America, p. 22* (StarMan Press 2019).
5 *Supra n. 2*, Privatopia.
[6] *Supra,* n.4, p. 4.
[7] *Community Next: 2020 and Beyond* (May 5, 2016). *A manifesto is a public declaration of intentions, opinions, objectives, or motives, as one issued by a government, sovereign, or organization. A white paper is an authoritative report or guide that informs readers concisely about a complex issue and presents the issuing body's philosophy on the matter. It is meant to help readers understand an issue, solve a problem, or make a decision.*

k. Restructure HOAs supplement released; join new website (2022)

To the concerned public and HOA members:

I am extending an invitation for the public at large, and in particular to members of HOAs across America, to join this FB group and keep abreast of critical developments and information regarding your membership and property rights in your castle, your home. Information not covered by the establishment, the self-proclaimed HOA educators.

In 2020 I released my 68-page *A Plan* ***Toward Restructuring the HOA Model of Governance,*** after 20 years of HOA reform activism. I also published a FAQ to answer questions regarding concern that a restructuring would damage the highly desirable HOA real estate package. "HOA" can also refer to the de facto local government of the real estate package, the condo or subdivision PUD. I believe that my plan would return HOAs to constitutional government with its protections for the rights and freedoms of citizens, severely lacking under your declaration of CC&Rs.

A detailed 27-page ***supplement,*** supporting the positions contained in the *Plan* and documenting the events and developments of a $22 million HOA in Arizona is now available.

Just visit the site, Restructure HOAs Plan, and click on the JOIN button. It's that easy.

Hope to see you there!

V. TABLE OF REFERENCES

The following references/links are not all inclusive of those contained within the Commentaries.

a. Cases

Arizona Biltmore Hotels Condo Assn v. Conlon (CACV 18-0709, June 23, 2020).
Brock v. Watergate Mobile Home, 502 So. 2d 1380 (Fla. 4th Dist. App. 1987).
Brooks v. Northglen, 141 S.W.3d 158 (Tex. 2004).
CAO v. Dorse, No. CA-CV 21-0275 (Ariz. Ct. App. 2022).
CBTW v. Twin Rivers (929 A.2d 1060, 2007).
Dublirer v. 2000 Linwood Avenue Owners Assn, N.J. Docket 069154 (N.J. 2014).
Gelb v. Casa Contenta HOA, CA-CV 09-0744, Ariz. App. Div. 1, Oct. 28, 2010).
Gelb v. DFBLS, CV 10-0371-PR (Ariz. 2011).
Kalway v. Calabria Ranch HOA LLC, et. al, 252 Ariz. 532 (2023).
Kosor v. Olympia Companies, NV No, 75669 (Dec. 31, 2020).
Marsh v. Alabama, 326 U.S. 501 (1946).
Mazdabrook Commons Homeowners Association v. Khan (N. J. 2012).
Midlake v. Cappuccio, 673 A.2d 340 (Pa.Super. 1996)
Shelly v. Kraemer, 334 U.S. 1 (1948).
Spanish Court Two Condominium Association v. Carlson, no. 115342 (IL 2014)
***State v. Glassel**, 116 P.3d 1193 (Ariz. 2005)*
Tarter v. Bendt, CV21-0049-PR (Ariz. 2021).
Timbs v. Indiana, no. 17-1091 (U.S. 2019).
Troon v. AZ DFBLS, LC2007-00598 (Maricopa County Superior Ct (Oct. 3, 2008). (Waugaman).

b. Statutes – laws

Declaration of Independence
US Constitution, 8th and14th amendments.
US Bill of Rights

AZ HB2774, Ariz. Sess. L. Ch. 105 (2010). (aka Take that George Bill).
AZ SB 1454, Ariz. Sess. L., Ch. 254 (2013).
FL Session Law, Ch. 229 (2023), "Homeowners' Associations Bill of Rights.

c. Secondary sources

- *A Bill Of Rights For Homeowners In Residential Community Associations, Lois Pratt and Samuel Pratt (1999)*
- *A Plan Toward Restructuring the HOA Model of Governance, George K. Staropoli, StarMan Publishing (2020).*
- *AARP HOA Bill of Rights, David A. Kahne, AARP Public Policy Institute (2006).*
- *Common Interest Communities: Private Governments and the Public Interest, Ch. 13, Stephen E. Barton & Carol J. Silverman, eds..*
- *Beyond Privatopia: Rethinking Residential Private Government, Evan McKenzie (Urban Inst. 2011)*
- *Community Associations: The Emergence and Acceptance of a Quiet Innovation in Housing, Donald R. Stabile (Greenwood Press 2000).*
- *Declaration of the Rights of Man and Citizen* (France, 1793).
- *Take Back Your Government; A Citizen's Guide to Grassroots Change, Morgan Carroll (Fulcrum Publishing 2011).*
- *Homeowners Bill of Rights, AHRC, Elizabeth McMahon (1997).*
- *The Constitution and Private Government: Toward the Recognition of Constitutional Rights in Private Residential Communities Fifty years After Marsh v.*

Alabama," Wm & Mary Bill of Rights, Steven Siegel, J., Vol. 6, Issue 2 (1998).

- *Establishing the New America of independent HOA principalities, George K. Staropoli, StarMan Publishing (2019).*
- *HOA Common Sense: rejecting private government, George K. Staropoli, StarMan Publishing (2013).*
- *The HOA-Land Nation Within America, George K. Staropoli, StarMan Publishing (2019).*
- *The Homes Association Handbook, Technical Bulletin #54, ULI (1964).*
- *Neighborhood Politics: Residential Community Associations in American Governance, Roger Jay Dilger, p. 160, New York Univ. Press (1992).*
- *Privatopia: Homeowners Associations and the Rise of Residential Private Governments, Evan McKenzie, Yale Univ. Press, 1994.*
- Report on Ventana Lakes POA *(murder trial)*
- *Restatement Third, Property: Servitudes (American Law Institute 2000).*
- *State of Arizona v. Glassel*, 116 P.3d 1193 (2005), review of Arizona No. CR-03-0022-AP, 2003.
- *Tate of Arizona v, Glassel*
- *The Twin Rivers Case: Of Homeowners Associations, Free Speech Rights And Privatized Mini-Governments, Paula A. Franzese and Steven Siegel, 5 RUTGERS J.L. & PUB. POL'Y 630 (2008)*

VI. GKS profile

George K. Staropoli Mr. Staropoli is a nationally recognized homeowners rights authority and advocate. Since April 2000 he has testified before legislative committees in Arizona, Florida and Nevada and his opinions and views have appeared in the national and local media. He has been quoted in Private Neighborhoods and the Transformation of Local Government (2005); AARP Policy Institute Homeowners Bill of Rights proposal (2006); acknowledged as a leading advocate in the Thomson – West legal treatise, California Common Interest Developments – Homeowner's Guide (2006); in Evan McKenzie's Beyond Privatopia (2011), and in Critical Housing Analysis (Vol. 1, Issue 1, 2019). Invited by Uniform Law Commission as an Observer participant in UCIOA revision committee, 2020.

In 2011 Mr. Staropoli's amicus curiae brief was accepted by the AZ Supreme Court in Gelb v. AZ DBFLS pertaining to the constitutionality of ALJ adjudication of HOA disputes. In 2013 he filed suit (Staropoli v. State of Arizona) against the State of Arizona for an unconstitutional bill, SB1454 and won

Emmy winning investigative reporter Ward Lucas (Neighbors at War!, 2012) writes about Staropoli saying, "*his knowledge is sophisticated . . . [he] has been able to articulate the deficiencies and the pending bombshells contained in the Legislature's denial of the obvious: that the HOA system is badly broken and in desperate need of an overhaul.*"

In 2000 Mr. Staropoli founded and is president of the nonprofit Citizens for Constitutional Local Government, Inc., Scottsdale, AZ, a nonprofit organization seeking to inform the legislators and public about common interest property issues and to expose the prevalent myths and propaganda about carefree living in an HOA. Citizens believes in supporting principles of American democracy.

He is a publisher of HOA issues and has authored: "Understanding the New America of HOA-Lands" (eBook, 2010), "Establishing the New America of independent HOA principalities" (2008), and he is author of HOA Common Sense: rejecting private government (eBook, 2013). George published an education course outline in 2015: The HOA-Land Nation Within America (2019). George also publishes on the internet.

Mr. Staropoli was a Vice President of an international securities brokerage firm, Shearson Hayden Stone (since merged and absorbed into Morgan Stanley Wealth Management); a member of the CEO Club, NY, NY; served as Treasurer and board member of a Penn. HOA; and served as a board member of the NYC Data Processing Assn and the Valley Citizens League, Phoenix, AZ. He holds a MS in Management from Polytechnic University, Brooklyn, NY (now NYU Tandon School - Polytechnic). Web pages: http://pvtgov.org; http://pvtgov.wordpress.com

VII. INDEX

Made in the USA
Las Vegas, NV
16 January 2024

84449905R00085